British Columbia Wild

A Natural History

British Columbia Wild

A Natural History

Tim Fitzharris

Text Assistance: **Audrey Fraggalosch**

Terrapin Press
Vancouver, B.C.

For Jim

CANADIAN CATALOGUING IN PUBLICATION DATA

Fitzharris, Tim 1948 -
  British Columbia Wild

Includes index.
Bibliography: p
ISBN 0-921151-00-4

1. Natural history — British Columbia. I.
Fraggalosch, Audrey, Christina, 1954 - II. Title.

QH106.2.B7F58 1986 508.711 C86-091157-8

Published by
TERRAPIN PRESS
1189 Johnston Road
White Rock, British Columbia
Telephone (604) 538-2212.
Printed in Vancouver, B.C. by
WAGNER & TELDON
Typeset in White Rock, B.C. by
PEREGRINE PRESS
Colour Separations in Vancouver, B.C. by
TRI-SCAN GRAPHICS
Marketing by
CAMERON, REYNOLDS, JONES & ASSOCIATES
Vancouver, B.C.

ACKNOWLEDGEMENTS

I am grateful to a number of people who assisted in the development of this book. Special appreciation goes to Yorke Edwards, the former director of the British Columbia Provincial Museum, for his critical editorial work on the manuscript. Wayne Campbell, Robert Cannings, Harold Hosford, and Robert Ogilvie, staff members of the provincial museum, also reviewed the text for scientific accuracy. Eileen Tuomaala provided valuable criticism of the manuscript in the final stages of editing. Fred Chapman was kind enough to permit me to use the two fine photographs appearing on pages 137 and 138. The maps were skillfully prepared by Doug Johnston with the assistance of the University of British Columbia's Geography Department.

Don Li-Leger provided valuable help in a number of photographic undertakings. Rob Butler and Susan Carlisle of the Canadian Wildlife Service assisted with field work carried out in the Kootenays. Jim Allen, David Denning, and Bob Sutherland of Ecosummer Canada and Bristol Foster facilitated shooting in the Queen Charlotte Islands. Bill McKay guided me to killer whales off Vancouver Island. Colin Knecht gave advice and field assistance for other photography carried out on Vancouver Island. On numerous occasions Cora Li-Leger supplied logistic support for expeditions afield. Jim Fitzharris worked as photographer's assistant on various excursions.

Special thanks to Audrey Fraggalosch for her determined and creative help both in the field and in researching and writing the text.

PRECEDING PAGES:
Short-billed dowitchers are among the many species of shorebirds that migrate along the British Columbia coast each spring and fall.

A common golden eye hen and her brood rest on a piece of driftwood.

RIGHT: An estimated one quarter of the world's population of bald eagles is found in British Columbia. Most nest in tall conifers along the coast.

CONTENTS

PREFACE

Left foot on the steep, rocky shore, right foot in the Zodiac, distance between increasing rapidly. I am trying to land on a group of rocky islets near Anthony Island at the southern end of the Queen Charlotte Archipelago. The swells moving in from the open Pacific are immense. One instant the large, inflatable boat is stationed reassuringly beside the landing spot, a moment later a surge of dark, cold water sweeps it 10 metres down the channel, bouncing it playfully into a sheer rock wall. I will soon learn the importance of timing.

My goal is to photograph northern sea lions. These animals stampede into the surf when a boat approaches their haulout sites—an impressive spectacle but one that prevents a photographer from getting any worthwhile pictures. I am attempting this tricky landing in order to approach the sunbathing herd on foot from the rear. I will have to scramble over an intervening maze of large rock shelves and outcrops, but with care I will be able to get within arm's length of the huge marine mammals whose attention is usually focused on the ocean. Any noise will be drowned out by the constant pounding of the sea and the gusting winds.

The adventure works out just about according to plan. I fall into the ocean, a pair of binoculars and one lens are digested by the salt water, the stalk is arduous but exhilarating, and I manage to get some exciting images.

A week later and approximately 900 kilometres to the southeast, I find myself sitting in the warm, morning sunshine of the Okanagan Valley watching a flock of cedar waxwings as it forages on squaw currants. My camera is set up, trained on one of the nearby shrubs should the waxwings decide to feed in my vicinity. In contrast to the Queen Charlotte Islands this is a serene, pastoral setting enlivened periodically by the bubbling song of a meadowlark or the whistle of a magpie. The ground is sparsely covered by tough clumps of bunchgrass and the soft, faded hues of sagebrush and rabbitbush are scattered here and there. The hillsides bristle with ponderosa pine and juniper.

Fortunately, I am able to position myself on a rock ledge that allows a sweeping view of the surrounding landscape. A warm slab of granite inclined at a 45 degree angle fits the contours of my backside comfortably, and soon I lapse into a rapturous state of semi-consciousness. My eyes are just glazing over when a movement on the rock face nearby catches my attention. The leathery, bulbous head of a rattlesnake slides cautiously out of a crack about an arm's length from my face. I can see the dark, heat-sensitive pits near the viper's nostrils that are used to guide the snake to a rodent hiding in the darkness. It spots me immediately, and a long, charcoal tongue flicks out, searching for a taste of my substance in the atmosphere.

The rattlesnake pauses only for a moment, and then the rest of its body emerges mechanically from the crevice and begins to slither down the rocks toward me. I am too groggy to scamper over the steep rocks to safety. Usually excitable and aggressive, this rattlesnake moves coolly toward me, apparently with sinister intention. Its rough, heavy body glides over one of my boots; the faint sensation generates a tingling impulse that sparks along both legs and then migrates upward to raise nervous prickles on my face and scalp. In a few moments the rattler winds its way into the bunchgrass and disappears.

Another week into the summer and 200 kilometres to the east a thunder-like crack resounds explosively in the humid air. I carefully set aside my greasy copy of *From Here to Eternity* and peer out one of the openings in the blind. Perched atop three storeys of rented scaffolding on a hill overlooking the Creston Valley, I have a fantastic view. The clouds do not look particularly ominous, and my attention shifts to the osprey nest directly in front of me about 20 metres away. One of the adults is hunkered over the three nestlings, catching a brief respite from its grueling parental duties.

Another sharp crack, clearly of non-meteorological origin, reverberates across the valley. A few moments later the other adult osprey labours into view bringing with it the cause of the mysterious sounds. From its talons hangs a dry, rotted piece of tree almost as long as a man and, at one end, as thick as a baseball bat. (Ospreys gather nesting material by diving on protruding snags, grasping them in their strong talons, and allowing their full weight and momentum to swing downward on the limb, snapping it off.) The raptor's long wings beat furiously as it fights to maintain altitude. Nearing the nest, it swoops to build up speed, sets its wings, and soars up to its waiting mate with the prize.

At once both adults awkwardly attempt to weave the unwieldy timber into their huge, coarse nest. In the process the nestlings receive a thorough clubbing. I wince every time one of them catches a blow, but they seem accustomed to the operation and are little harmed. After shooting almost a roll of film on the incident I return to my reading, and the ospreys settle in for a nap.

These are just a few of the experiences that I enjoyed while working on the photographs for this book. Presented here, in what I hope is an interesting and easily understood way, is an overview of the province's natural history. British Columbia's wild places are incredibly diverse and ever changing. Some are abundant, others are fragile, unique, and quite restricted. Above all this book is intended to celebrate the natural beauty of these places and plea for their preservation.

Tim Fitzharris
May 1986

FOLLOWING PAGES: A small herd of northern sea lions churns up a bull kelp bed near Pachena Point on Vancouver Island.

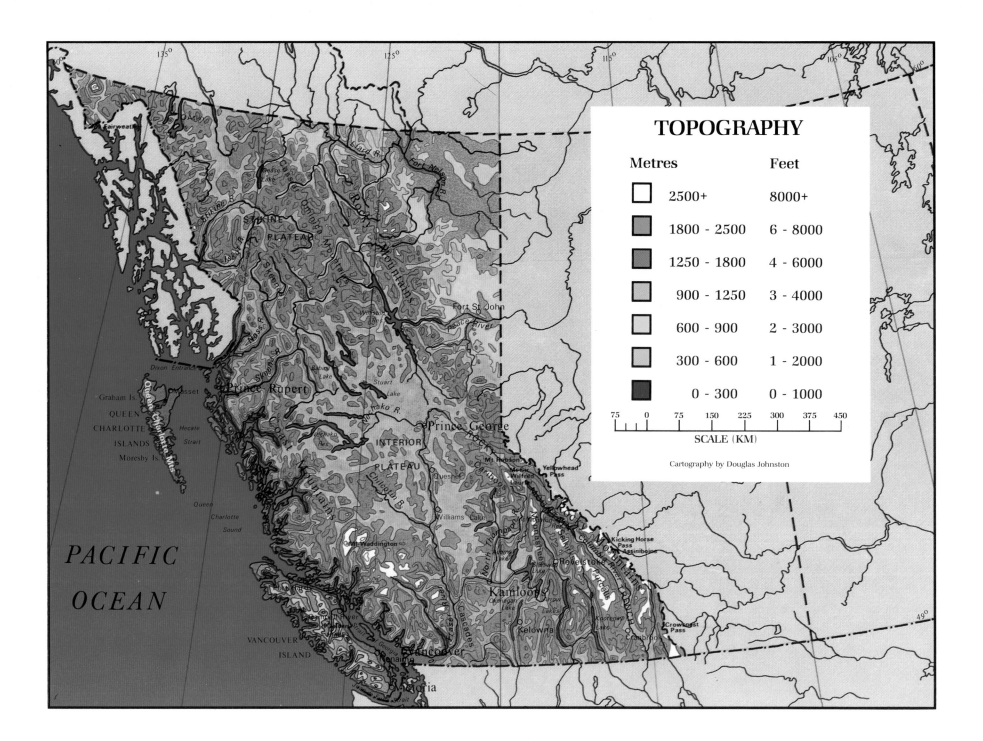

TOPOGRAPHY

Metres	Feet
2500+	8000+
1800 - 2500	6 - 8000
1250 - 1800	4 - 6000
900 - 1250	3 - 4000
600 - 900	2 - 3000
300 - 600	1 - 2000
0 - 300	0 - 1000

75   0   75   150   225   300   375   450

SCALE (KM)

Cartography by Douglas Johnston

A LAND OF CONTRASTS

The natural history of British Columbia is by and large a product of the region's geography and climate. The province is roughly rectangular in shape. Vancouver, the metropolitan centre, is situated in the extreme southwest corner. Northward for 1600 kilometres stretches a vast hinterland, in area about equal to England, France, and Italy combined, but supporting a population only 1½ percent as large. From the jagged Pacific coastline to the Alberta border the province measures about 700 kilometres. Over 90 percent of the land is mountainous with 75 percent of it more than 1000 metres above sea level. Forests cover almost two-thirds of the land surface; most of the remainder is given over to rock and barrens, icefields, lakes, and rivers. Only five percent is used for agriculture.

British Columbia's topography is astoundingly diverse. Aside from the offshore islands it consists fundamentally of three, parallel, geologic regions running in a north/south direction. On the west are the Coast Mountains, to the east lies the Rocky Mountain system, and sandwiched between is a vast, complex region of plateaus, mountains, and hills.

Offshore Islands

The first landforms encountered on British Columbia's western edge are islands, literally thousands of them, varying in size from tiny, unnamed rock reefs to Vancouver Island with an area of more than 25,000 square kilometres. Two insular systems predominate. The Queen Charlotte Archipelago, lying 100 kilometres offshore about halfway up the coast, consists of two large islands, Graham and Moresby, and about 150 smaller ones. Comprising the second group are Vancouver Island and the adjacent Gulf Islands. Separated from the mainland by a series of narrow straits, they lie in the extreme south of the province.

Sitting on the outer edge of the continental shelf, the Queen

Charlotte Islands are the most isolated land mass in the country. Unrestrained, ponderous, the Pacific Ocean thunders against the archipelago's western wall, a mountain buttress that emerges precipitously from the dark seas. The Skidegate Plateau occupies much of the north-central region of the Queen Charlottes while the eastern side is coastal lowland. A broad, sandy beach resulting from the vigorous wave action of Hecate Strait on glacial deposits stretches almost the entire length of Graham Island while Moresby Island's shoreline is fissured by rocky coves and inlets.

During the last Ice Age the warming effect of the ocean insulated the islands from the extreme glaciation which ravaged the rest of the province. As a result many species of plants and animals found refuge here and have since evolved along a distinct and specialized pathway. Together with some of the islands' other unique aspects—the isolation from the rest of the continent, a mild climate of heavy rains, unabated winds and frequent driving storms, a gnarled landscape upholstered with luxuriant forests, the incredible richness of the surrounding marine environments, and the sparsity of human settlement— one discovers a misty, enchanting land whose natural character finds no counterpart elsewhere in the world.

Some 220 kilometres to the south lies Vancouver Island. The largest island on the west coast of North America, it is shaped like a thick, lumpy cigar and measures about 450 kilometres long and 130 kilometres wide. Nestled in a protective notch of the continental land mass, the island is walled in by the towering mountains of the British Columbia mainland and Washington's

OPPOSITE LEFT: The spectacular Coast Mountains as reflected in the stillness of the Pitt River.

OPPOSITE RIGHT: Mussels and barnacles exposed by the receding tide crowd the rocky, serrated coastline of Pacific Rim National Park on Vancouver Island.

LEFT: Ice flows clog the Fraser River near Williams Lake.

Olympic Peninsula. These barriers not only shield it from extreme, continental weather systems, but work to keep the plant and animal communities of the Pacific coast separate from those of the interior regions of the province. Vancouver Island is further insulated from mainland influences by the relatively benign Juan de Fuca Strait to the south and the Strait of Georgia (clogged by the Gulf Islands), Johnstone Strait, and Queen Charlotte Strait to the east. The island's northern coast and most of its western coast lie open to the pounding waves and violent weather of the Pacific Ocean.

This outer coastline is a chaotic, convoluted mass of rocky islands, precipitous headlands, and deep, twisting fiords, some of which penetrate more than halfway across the island. Here public road construction has been impractical, and the handful of human settlements is accessible by boat, floatplane, or logging roads. Lowlands stretching the length of the inner coast are, like the Gulf Islands lying offshore, more hospitable, both in climate and topography. In general, however, Vancouver Island's terrain is mountainous. A jumble of peaks and ranges covers most of the land away from the sea. Few of the mountains rise above 2100 metres, and by mainland standards they are decidedly puny. Nevertheless, they distinguish the landscape with an aura of rugged wilderness. Deep valleys slash randomly through these ranges, some extending across the island to merge with the fiords of the outer coast.

Coast Mountains

Separated from these two island groups by deep, glacial gouged, submarine troughs, called the Hecate and Georgia Depressions, are the magnificent Coast Mountains of the British Columbia mainland. The coastline itself is shredded and fissured by deep fiords and broad inlets; it becomes in many places a bewildering maze of offshore islands and channels. The headlands are rugged, heavily treed, and rise steeply out of the sea. Faced with such obstacles, the coastal highway, broken several times by the necessity of ferry transport, extends fitfully from Vancouver to Lund, a distance of only 240 kilometres. Here it ends abruptly, and the remaining 1400 kilometres of British Columbia's western edge must be serviced by boat or plane. At Prince Rupert, a shipping terminal halfway up the coast, a road slithers through the mountain barrier following the Skeena River valley from the interior region out to the sea. But the orientation of this transportation corridor is decidedly east/west, and this highway does little to alter the isolated aspect of the extensive coastline.

Beginning at the Yukon border and stretching almost to the United States, the Coast Mountains stand as the province's western superstructure. The system averages some 300 kilometres in width. Coastal fiords cut deeply into the mountains in many places, sometimes even channeling the sea past a range's summit line, creating a stunningly compressed juxtaposition of alpine, forest, and marine habitats. The northernmost coastal mountains are the St. Elias Range. Relatively young and little dulled by erosion, their fog-shrouded peaks are the province's most rugged and precipitous, with 4600 metre Mount Fairweather laying claim as the highest. This region lies within the steely influence of arctic weather systems and is subjected to an unending onslaught of ice and snow.

In general, elevations decrease southward until reaching a wild, rugged zone opposite Vancouver Island—the topographic heartland of the Coast Range—where heights again attain more than 3000 metres. The highest, Mount Waddington, is 4016 metres. Glaciation carved and chiselled the mountain sides above the 2000 metre level bestowing on much of the terrain a gaunt, towering, flinty magnificence. Lower mountains, composed mostly of granite, were completely buried in the ice, and their peaks were rounded smooth by the incredible force of

OPPOSITE: The Gulf Islands in the Strait of Georgia at sunset.

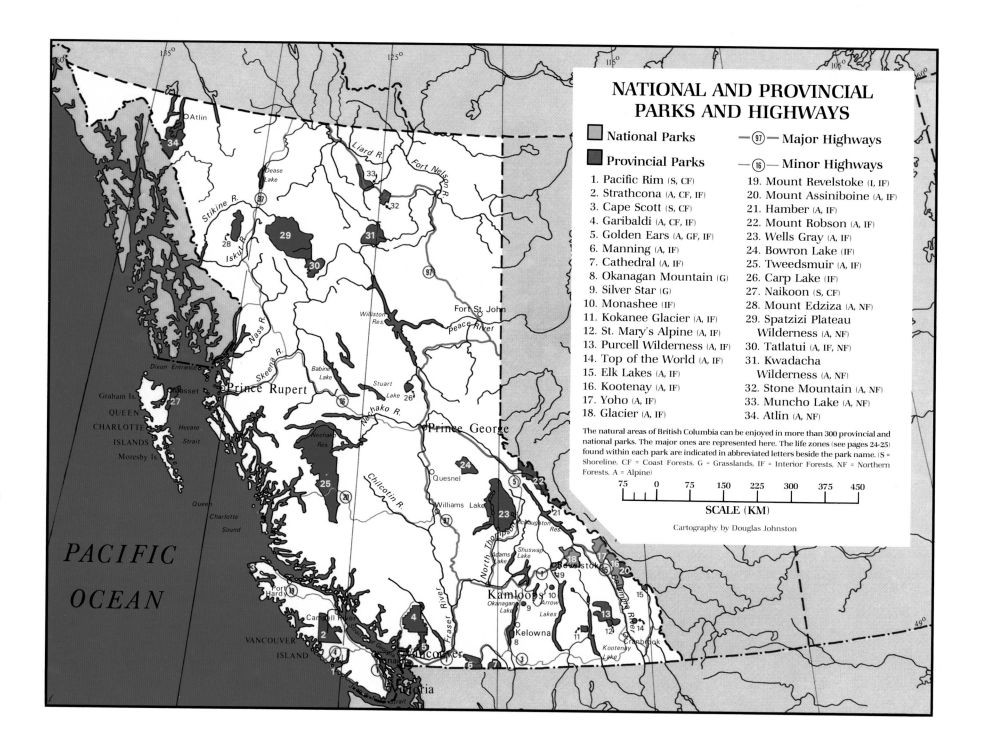

NATIONAL AND PROVINCIAL PARKS AND HIGHWAYS

■ National Parks   —97— Major Highways

■ Provincial Parks   —16— Minor Highways

1. Pacific Rim (S, CF)
2. Strathcona (A, CF, IF)
3. Cape Scott (S, CF)
4. Garibaldi (A, CF, IF)
5. Golden Ears (A, GF, IF)
6. Manning (A, IF)
7. Cathedral (A, IF)
8. Okanagan Mountain (G)
9. Silver Star (G)
10. Monashee (IF)
11. Kokanee Glacier (A, IF)
12. St. Mary's Alpine (A, IF)
13. Purcell Wilderness (A, IF)
14. Top of the World (A, IF)
15. Elk Lakes (A, IF)
16. Kootenay (A, IF)
17. Yoho (A, IF)
18. Glacier (A, IF)

19. Mount Revelstoke (I, IF)
20. Mount Assiniboine (A, IF)
21. Hamber (A, IF)
22. Mount Robson (A, IF)
23. Wells Gray (A, IF)
24. Bowron Lake (IF)
25. Tweedsmuir (A, IF)
26. Carp Lake (IF)
27. Naikoon (S, CF)
28. Mount Edziza (A, NF)
29. Spatzizi Plateau
     Wilderness (A, NF)
30. Tatlatui (A, IF, NF)
31. Kwadacha
     Wilderness (A, NF)
32. Stone Mountain (A, NF)
33. Muncho Lake (A, NF)
34. Atlin (A, NF)

The natural areas of British Columbia can be enjoyed in more than 300 provincial and national parks. The major ones are represented here. The life zones (see pages 24-25) found within each park are indicated in abbreviated letters beside the park name. (S = Shoreline, CF = Coast Forests, G = Grasslands, IF = Interior Forests, NF = Northern Forests, A = Alpine)

| 75 | 0 | 75 | 150 | 225 | 300 | 375 | 450 |

SCALE (KM)

Cartography by Douglas Johnston

the moving glaciers. Extensive ice fields, remnants of the last period of glaciation, are still found throughout the highest regions of the Coast Range. Due to its colder latitude much more of the north is buried perennially under ice and snow. South of the Alaskan Panhandle, the seaward terrain is largely rain soaked, fog bound, and thickly forested. The eastern slopes receive less precipitation, and consequently the vegetation is not so luxuriant.

The Coast Mountains end at the Fraser River where they meet the Cascade Mountains, an extensive, volcanically active system which extends all the way to California. The Cascades occupy a significant portion of southern British Columbia, being bounded on the east by the Similkameen River and on the west by Cultus Lake, and stretching northward in a diminishing triangular shape for 140 kilometres. The area is composed of much sedimentary rock which has been eroded and rounded by the great ice sheet that had its southern terminus here 10,000 years ago. The Cascades contain some relatively high, rocky peaks; broad, elevated, subalpine meadows and ridges, and deeply cut valleys with numerous lakes, beaver ponds, and streams. The flora is rich and is distributed in rather complex patterns owing to the variety of elevation and the position of the range itself lying between the wet coastal zone and the dry interior regions.

Creating another significantly different adjunct to the Coast Mountain zone is the Fraser lowland. Over millions of years the river has carried eroded particles from interior regions, in the process carving steep, rocky canyons through the mountains and sculpturing a broad, flat valley that now extends from the present river's mouth to the mountain community of Hope situated 150 kilometres upstream. The river laid down its burden of sediments creating a fertile plain, in places over 500

Moose are found in forested regions throughout much of the province, particularly the northern forests.

metres thick. The process continues. Each year the delta reaches further into the Strait of Georgia, sometimes as much as two and a half metres, as the river deposits some 20 million tonnes more of sand, silt, clay, and gravel. The Fraser lowland is the most densely populated region in the province and has been drastically altered from its natural state by intensive agricultural and industrial development. Nevertheless, the estuary and surrounding region comprise an exceedingly rich if rapidly declining habitat for wildlife of many varieties.

Interior System

By far the largest geologic division in the province is the Interior System, a vast, rugged terrain of varied landforms. Most of this rolling landscape lies at an elevation between 600 and 1200 metres, but a great portion is disrupted by mountains, highlands, dry valleys, and many small lakes, streams, and rivers. Glacial and volcanic activity have left their distinctive marks on the countryside in many places. The ice flows carved horn shaped peaks and fluted ridges out of the mountain tops, created hanging valleys and lofty, pristine tarns, scraped out broad, elongated depressions, and left empty riverbeds and wide meltwater channels. Lava flows have dappled the terrain with cones, mountainous humps, and flat topped domes and built the precipitous rock ridges of the Spectrum Range in gaudy hues of red, yellow, and purple.

The northern third of the Interior System is primarily mountainous. Flanking the Coast Range on the western side are the Stikine Plateau and Skeena Mountains; in the far eastern third are the Cassiar-Omineca Ranges, and sandwiched amidst these land forms is the Spatzizi Plateau. Most of this area lies within the arctic watershed. The Peace and Liard Rivers and their tributaries carry water eastward, joining the Mackenzie River on its northward flow. Several smaller watercourses in the western region cut through the Coastal Range, meeting the heads of long, inreaching fiords to carry runoff out to the Pacific Ocean. Almost uninhabited except for a handful of mining and forestry communities, this northern region is for the most part true wilderness—an isolated, broken landscape jumbled into an arresting disarray of peaks and plateaus, assaulted by a harsh, cold climate, clothed by a monotony of evergreen forests, and for much of the year locked within a brittle shield of snow and ice.

Particularly remote and unknown are the northern reaches of the Cassiar-Omineca Ranges. Except for the lone thread of the Alaskan Highway, this wilderness is inaccessible by road—a world of long, metal nights quieted by murmuring streams, wind-rushed forests, and the patter of the wolf pack. Here is evidence of the land's intractable durability, of irresistible forces working unmindful of human enterprise.

A broad plateau forms the central region of the Interior System. Here the countryside rolls endlessly, a terrain dotted with many lakes and laced with streams and rivers that have carved through the land in many places, creating channels with terraced, near vertical cliffs. The area is dominated by the Fraser River. The only major watercourse totally within the province, it rises in the Rockies, loops westward and is joined by the Nechako River at Prince George. Here it streams southward for nearly 500 kilometres, its tributaries from both sides draining the plateau country. East of the river lies the Cariboo—a dry, sunny, lake-stippled region of rolling meadows, aspen groves, and pine forests. West of the Fraser is the Chilcotin region, similar in character to the Cariboo, but less settled and becoming more rugged as the terrain blends into the uplands of the Coast Mountains. Although unsuitable for sedentary agriculture, the grasslands of the plateau system support widespread cattle grazing; forestry is also important, and numerous small communities based on these activities are scattered throughout the area.

OPPOSITE: Harassed by a crow, an immature bald eagle perches on a snag while looking for prey like the scoters in the distance.

The Interior System becomes progressively narrower in its southern reaches. Here the significant topographical features are broad valleys—the Fraser, Thompson, South Thompson, Okanagan, Nicola, and Similkameen. This is semi-desert country, hot and dry; the air is crystalline; the skies are laser clear for much of the year. Many lakes are found throughout the region, the larger ones like Adams, Shuswap, and Okanagan, twisting snake-like through long valleys, their metallic blue waters accenting the tawny, textured landscape. The valley bottoms and lower slopes are clothed with the pale, grey-green hues of sagebrush, bunchgrass, and cactus. Patches of ponderosa pine and juniper are salted about the benches and rocky hills. Aided by irrigation, much of the lowland is now an extremely fertile, fruit growing region, quilted by geometric arrangements of vineyards and orchards. The relatively balmy climate and sunny skies also have made tourism an important local industry. With its rattlesnakes and prairie falcons, sagebrush flats, tumbleweeds, and stark, eroded gulches and canyons, the dry southern interior exudes an aura of the old west, a flavour as unique and savoury as any in the province.

The Eastern Mountain System

British Columbia's eastern frontier is guarded for much of its length by an intimidating barrier of mountain ranges, the highest and most extensive being the relatively young and sharply honed Rocky Mountains. Buffering the Rockies from the Interior System are the Columbia Mountains, made up of a number of lesser ranges running parallel in a north/south direction. Moving eastward across the broad base of the Columbia Mountains, one encounters in succession the rounded, thickly forested slopes of the Monashees, the higher, more rugged peaks of the Selkirks, and towering alongside the Rockies themselves are the Purcells, in places sharply pinnacled, elsewhere massive and blunt. Forming the northern

apex of the Columbia Mountains triangle are the Cariboo Mountains, a large, wild pocket of high, jagged, icebound peaks. The tallest, Mount Sir Wilfred Laurier, soars some 3500 metres into the clouds. The precipitous aspects of these ranges are heightened by the picturesque valleys which slice into the heart of the formations. A land of magnificent scenery with a network of good roads, it is frequented increasingly by both summer and winter recreation seekers.

The eastern edge of the Columbia Mountains is marked dramatically by a magnificent valley known as the Rocky Mountain Trench. It runs uninterrupted almost the entire length of the province. A smooth, sunken corridor kilometres wide in places, it stretches arrow-like from horizon to horizon, so formal in its design one cannot help but speculate about the mathematical principles underlying its origin. Its lowest topography is punctuated through most of its length by rivers and ribbon-like lakes. The Columbia River, one of the province's major waterways, follows the trench for some distance, gathering melted water from the Columbia Icefields and Selkirk glaciers before sweeping around the northern end of the Selkirk Range and heading south again through the Arrow Lakes, crossing the United States border to empty eventually into the Pacific Ocean. Most of the trench is thickly upholstered by conifers, patterned extensively in some areas by the light green squares of second growth timber—the calculated work of the forest industrialists.

The towering walls of the Rockies roll steeply out of this trench, building a skyline of ice-crowned peaks and barren, hard-spined ridges. Broken by only a few passes like the Kicking Horse, Crowsnest, and Yellowhead which are used as rail and road corridors, the Rockies straddle the boundary with Alberta to the midway point of the province. North of this the ranges continue their northwestward projection well into the interior of the province while the border angles due north, in the process

claiming for British Columbia a huge area of the Great Plains. The Rockies are composed mostly of eroded sedimentary rock—upthrust, folded, bent, or broken depending on the initial manner of formation and subsequently sculpted by the grinding imprint of glaciers. The contour of the slopes and peaks exhibits much variation, from the spire-like configuration of Mount Assiniboine to the monumental fortress structure of Mount Robson, the Rockies' tallest peak at close to 4000 metres.

In the northern half of the province, the eastern slopes of the Rockies taper into a region of rounded foothills, which in turn settle out and fade into the flat spread of North America's Great Plains. This elevated table land occupies nearly ten percent of British Columbia's surface area. As the only geologic division lying outside of the province's curtain of mountains, it is subjected to many continental influences. Its climate, flora, and fauna are similar to those found in the forested plains north of the prairies. Most of the countryside is thickly clothed with white and black spruce, part of the vast swath of northern, or boreal, forest that stretches from coast to coast. A relatively small area in the far northeastern corner of the province is open to grain farming, interrupted here and there by stands of aspen, birch, willow, and balsam poplar. In the warmer seasons it is enlivened by a riot of colourful wildflowers and eastern songbirds.

Climate

It is the effect of climate on the province's geologic matrix that determines the nature of the land's covering vegetation and in turn the make-up of the animal communities. Tahsis is a tiny town on the outer coast of Vancouver Island. Each year every square centimetre of this soggy community—log dumps, piers, gardens, rooftops, roadways, crickets, snails, gulls, mailmen—is drowned by over three metres of rain. Meanwhile, in the

Poisonous fly agaric mushrooms grow among kinnikinnick groundcover.

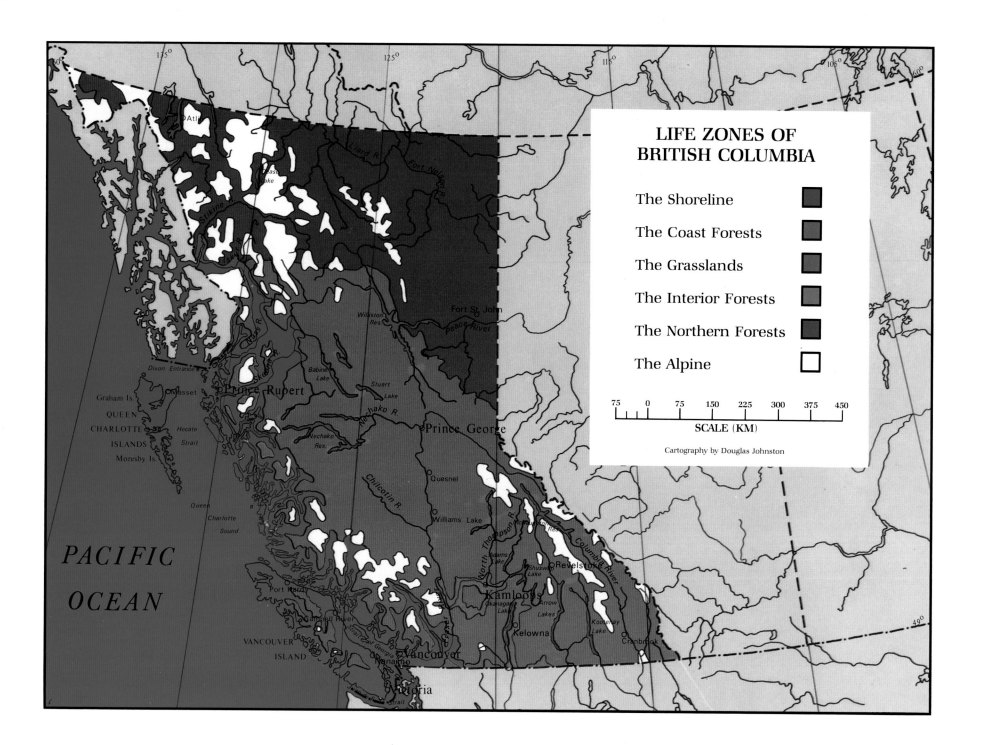

LIFE ZONES OF BRITISH COLUMBIA

The Shoreline

The Coast Forests

The Grasslands

The Interior Forests

The Northern Forests

The Alpine

75   0   75   150   225   300   375   450

SCALE (KM)

Cartography by Douglas Johnston

PACIFIC

OCEAN

Graham Is.
QUEEN
CHARLOTTE
ISLANDS
Moresby Is.

Hecate
Strait

Dixon Entrance

Masset

Prince Rupert

Queen
Charlotte
Sound

VANCOUVER
ISLAND

Port Hardy

Campbell River

Nanaimo

Vancouver

Victoria

Atlin

Peace
Lake

Stikine

Liard R.

Fort Nelson R.

Williston
Res.

Fort St. John

Peace River

Babine
Lake

Skeena R.

Nass R.

Stuart
Lake

Nechako R.

Nechako
Res.

Prince George

Chilcotin R.

Quesnel

Williams Lake

North Thompson R.

Adams
Lake

Shuswap
Lake

Revelstoke

Columbia River

Kamloops

Okanagan
Lake

Arrow
Lakes

Kootenay
Lake

Kelowna

Cranbrook

60°   135°   125°   115°   105°   60°

49°

province's interior the bustling city of Kamloops is as dry as parchment, receiving less than 15 centimetres of precipitation annually. In January Vancouver's mean temperature is a balmy, flower-growing, +3° C, but in the province's far north Fort Nelson shivers in the iron grip of an unrelenting winter, its mean temperature standing at -24° C. British Columbia's extreme climatic variation, the greatest in Canada, is mostly a product of its diverse topography.

The province's precipitation pattern is generated primarily by weather systems blowing in from the Pacific Ocean. When these warm winds collide with the outer coast, the abundant moisture carried in the air begins to fall as rain. As the air mass is forced upward by the mountains, it is further cooled, and precipitation increases dramatically. The outer coastal regions record annual average rainfalls in the 250 centimetre range, while higher slopes further inland may receive twice this amount. By the time the air swirls past the first peaks it has dried considerably. As the weather systems roll over each successive range of mountains, the air becomes drier and drier. Given British Columbia's topography of parallel, north/south running mountain ranges, a distinctive pattern of alternating wet and dry belts emerges. The windward sides of the mountains are zones of heavy rainfall and consequent luxuriant vegetation. The leeward slopes receive lighter precipitation, and they are less thickly forested, in fact some of these rain shadow zones are so dry as to be classed as semi-desert. Precipitation declines eastward as each new range of mountains wrings its quota of moisture from the air. The province's precipitation pattern is relatively simple, but the picture is disrupted from time to time and from place to place by regional topographic anomalies and regular invasions of arctic and continental weather systems.

Temperature also has a critical impact on plant growth. The province's geographic position brings it under the influence of air masses warmed by the North Pacific Drift, a system of ocean currents originating in the tropics that bathes the entire coastline in balmy temperatures. Most of this region experiences more than 200 frost free days per year compared with less than 60 for much of the rest of the province. Generally, overall temperatures begin to fall as one moves inland away from the ocean's warming effect. In northern areas this change is influenced by arctic weather systems and higher elevation, where, for each rise of 300 metres, the temperature drops one degree centigrade. The coldest spot in the province then would seem to be a mountain top far from the coast near the Yukon border—not the best place for a watermelon patch. For precisely the opposite reasons Victoria, the capital city, lays claim as the province's hot spot.

Life Zones

Throughout British Columbia the plant communities are comprised of species adapted to the climatic and geologic constraints of their environments—ferns and mosses proliferate in the warm, wet forests of the coast, cacti and antelope bush cling tenaciously to the baked, arid soils of the interior grasslands. Each of these plant communities is characterized by a few dominant plants, usually trees, which are adapted to similar conditions. Growing in association with them are certain shrubs, ferns, herbs, mosses, and fungi. By supplying food, cover, and reproductive habitat this vegetative pattern in turn determines the type and abundance of animal life. All of these associated organisms, both plant and animal, when considered as a group, represent a life zone. It is important to keep in mind when you are in the field that the boundaries between such zones are natural and therefore often indistinct. Localized influences of climate, soil, and topography may create micro-habitats that are not characteristic of a zone's overall pattern.

Scientists recognize 12 distinct life zones in British Columbia. For reasons of simplification this book combines some of these zones and presents six major divisions: the shoreline, the coast forests, the grasslands, the interior forests, the northern forests, and the alpine. Each of these life zones is described more fully in subsequent chapters.

OPPOSITE LEFT: *Alpine fir and mountain hemlock grow at higher elevations throughout the province's interior forests zone.*

OPPOSITE RIGHT: *Licorice ferns are found in the dry coastal woodlands of southern Vancouver Island—part of the coast forests zone.*

RIGHT: *In the province's dry interior, balsam root sunflowers bloom during May among ponderosa pine woods, a transitional community that displays characteristics of both the grasslands zone and the interior forests zone.*

CHAPTER 1

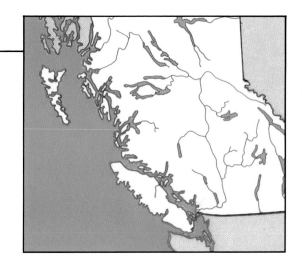

THE SHORELINE

Whether shrouded in fog or glistening in sunlight, British Columbia's 25,000 kilometre coastline is breathtaking—a maze of countless islands, deep penetrating fiords, and high, steep headlands. In many areas the sea breaks against a backdrop of towering, ice-crowned mountains and plunging slopes overgrown with magnificent forests. Most of the outer coastal beaches are a jumble of jagged granite that batters the incoming surf into foam and shooting spray. The sheltered inner coast is more subdued in character with its multitude of quiet coves, winding waterways, and small islands. In scattered locations there are fantastic sea stacks and caves carved by the Pacific, long stretches of grey, hard-packed sand, and pockets of cobblestone beach. Just as spectacular as the landscape is the amazing diversity of life found in tidal areas and offshore waters.

Intertidal Zone

The intertidal zone is a unique world where plants and animals have adapted to survive and even to flourish in a habitat that is sometimes saltwater and sometimes terrestrial. It encompasses that part of the shore between the high tide and low tide marks. Usually twice each day the tide ebbs and floods, bathing the intertidal zone and all its weirdly configured and hungry creatures with an incredibly nutritious, saltwater soup. Under optimum conditions a single litre of British Columbia seawater may contain as many as 50,000 microscopic organisms. Plankton, as they are called collectively, is the basis of every marine food chain. It is eaten by a host of animals large and small—from shrimp to blue whales. The smallest creatures become food for larger predatory animals which may be eaten by even bigger predators still higher in the food chain. In the intertidal zone, one finds a kaleidoscopic collection of unusual animals, many that feast on the banquet served with each incoming tide, others that prey on these planktonic grazers, and all of them adapted to survive the dangers that threaten once the water recedes, and they are exposed to the air and sun.

Bathed with sea water for only brief periods each day, the high tide zone is the least hospitable of tidal areas. Its resident animals must survive the battering of waves, long periods of drying, limited access to the planktonic food resources, and great fluctuations in temperature and water salinity. To avoid being tossed about by waves or carried off by a hungry predator, most cling tenaciously to their segment of rocky real estate. Barnacles, one of the most common animals of the high tide zone, are anchored with cement as durable as the rock itself; blue mussels hold on with a fibrous network of tough hairs; limpets plaster themselves onto the rocks with airtight suction. Like most of the high tide creatures, these sedentary animals have hard shells which protect them from shore predators and dehydration once the tide recedes. Further shelter from sun and hungry eyes is provided by thick, slippery mats of rockweed and sea lettuce that may cover much of the beach at low tide. This jungle of vegetation is also a refuge for a more active cast of animals: a variety of crabs, several species of snail-like whelks, and strange, finger-sized animals with long, flattened bodies and seven pairs of legs called isopods.

Flooded with plankton rich seawater for most of the day, the low tide zone harbours an abundance of animals of amazing colours and patterns and often intimidating configurations. Brilliant, five-armed blood stars; flower-shaped, green anemones; leathery segmented, black chitons; and spiky, red sea urchins crowd the tide pools and rocks. Life here is often as bizarre as it appears to the eye. A large, conspicuous predator, the purple seastar, uses its powerful, suction arms to open a clam or mussel and then extrudes its sac-like stomach through its mouth and into the innards of its victim to digest it on the spot. Another graceful, seemingly delicate predator is the red anemone. It ambushes crabs, snagging them in its waving tentacles, chewing them up, and spitting out the leftover shell in less than fifteen minutes.

When the tide is out many terrestrial mammals and birds invade the beach to feed on the sea life that is uncovered. Black bears, mink, and raccoons rummage about the loose rocks and cobblestones for crabs, while river otters fish the shallows for sculpins and blennies. Flocks of sandpipers and dowitchers undulate above exposed mud and sand flats, now and then landing abruptly to probe for worms, fish eggs, tiny snails, and clams. Mobs of glaucous-winged gulls squabble and scream over broken clams or decaying fish. Lanky great blue herons stand immobile in the tidal pools, waiting for fish to come within striking range, and black oystercatchers chisel mussels off the bottom with their scarlet bills. Bald eagles ogle the entire scene, regularly taking a duck or coot, snagging a salmon from the water's surface, or tearing at carrion washed up on the beach.

Offshore Waters

In the open water beyond the intertidal zone, animal activity on the surface hints at the abundant life of the depths. Scoters, mergansers, cormorants, and grebes forage through the kelp beds and on submerged reefs for small fish and molluscs. The abundance of food attracts harbor seals, California and northern sea lions, and sometimes even elephant seals. Their primary natural predator is the killer whale, or orca. Travelling in small groups, killer whales are seen more readily in British Columbia's offshore waters than elsewhere in the world. Grey whales frequently are sighted as they migrate along the coast on their 16,000 kilometre journey between California and Alaska. They are easily recognized by their immense size and row of dorsal humps. Once plentiful, humpback whales and sea otters were hunted to near extinction during the last century and are rarely found off the province's coast today.

PAGE 28: *A wild stretch of rocky beach on Cleland Island near Tofino.*

OPPOSITE: *A great blue heron lands a sculpin from a tidal pool. The heron will flip the fish around to prevent the spiny fins from harming its throat.*

Harbor seals are found all along the British Columbia coast. Their mottled coats camouflage remarkably well with the barnacle-patched, algae-covered rocks that serve as their haulout places. On land harbor seals are clumsy and invariably remain within a quick swim, scramble, or roll of the water's edge. Once under water the harbor seal's heart rate slows, its nostrils close tightly, and its pupils dilate to adjust to the dark depths. Its body is streamlined and smoothed by layers of blubber that insulate it from the cold water. Powerful hind flippers propel it swiftly and gracefully while subtle movements of the body and front flippers steer it unerringly through jungles of kelp and over rocky shoals.

At high tide harbor seals do most of their foraging. Fish comprise 99 percent of their diet with molluscs and crustaceans making up the remainder. As the tide recedes, the seals crawl onto rocky islets to snooze and digest the food caught during the previous tidal movement.

In late summer and autumn mating occurs in shallow waters or on haulout areas. Females usually give birth to a single pup on isolated beaches in spring. For the first few days the pups do little but float about examining the world through large, curious eyes. In a week they gain considerable strength, swimming ashore and even diving to suckle from their mother who floats vertically in the water. Harbor seals are shy creatures, and their rookeries and haulouts need protection from human disturbance.

RIGHT: The chinook is prey for harbor seals. Like other salmon it dies almost immediately after spawning in coastal streams. Gulls, ravens, mink, and raccoons will feed on its carcass.

OPPOSITE: A harbor seal surfaces near a kelp-draped islet. These marine mammals can remain submerged for over 20 minutes if necessary.

The offshore waters of British Columbia support an estimated population of 350 killer whales, or orcas. These highly social, marine mammals travel in small, extended family groups, or pods, generally numbering between eight and 30 individuals. One of the most impressive features of a swimming pod is the size of the dominant bull's dorsal fin which sometimes stands taller than a man.

A bull killer whale is occasionally more than nine metres long and weighs up to 5.5 tonnes. Despite their immense size, orcas are surprisingly agile and engage in a number of spectacular surface manoeuvres. These include spy-hopping (rising vertically out of the water), breaching (leaping completely out of the water), and tail lobbing (slamming the flukes on the water surface). Beach rubbing is another curious behaviour. For reasons not yet fully understood, members of a pod sometimes gather near a short stretch of pebble beach to rub themselves on the smooth stones, often with their bodies well out of the water.

Killer whales hunt a variety of animals—fish, seals, sea lions, dolphins, large sea birds, and even other whales. Resident pods in British Columbia feed almost exclusively on salmon while the diet of transient whales is comprised of mostly marine mammals. Although killer whales are extremely powerful and fearless carnivores, no humans have ever been harmed despite numerous incidents in which man would have been easy prey.

OPPOSITE: A misty evening settles on a cobblestone beach in the Queen Charlotte Islands.

RIGHT: A killer whale swims in Johnstone Strait off northeastern Vancouver Island. This area is one of the best places in the world to observe orcas.

One of the richest biological regions of the province is the estuary at the mouth of the Fraser River. As in most estuaries, plant growth is prolific due to the varied and constant supply of nutrients delivered by both river runoff and tidal action. Along the shore are extensive stretches of tidal marsh which provide breeding areas, food, and protective cover for fish, birds, and mammals. Eelgrass beds found beyond the low water mark are stable habitat for crabs and other invertebrates, spawning sites for herring, and nurseries for salmon. Diving ducks and brant geese feed on the plants themselves. The waters offshore are rich in seaweeds and plankton, a continuously available food source especially important for primary consumers of the food chain such as clams, snails, mussels, shrimp, isopods, and amphipods.

The Fraser River estuary is renowned for its magnificent bird life. Located on the Pacific Flyway, the area is visited by millions of waterfowl and shorebirds during spring and fall migration. Flocks of sandpipers numbering in the thousands perform spectacular aerial displays, called 'helioscoping', in which all the birds alternately flash their white bellies and dark backs in a perfectly synchronised, rhythmic series. Such manoeuvres are believed to confuse falcons and hawks which prey on them. The estuary is Canada's most important wintering area for waterfowl, and during colder months it is home for thousands of snow geese that fly in from Siberia.

Thousands of snow geese spend the winter on the Fraser River estuary feeding on the roots of aquatic vegetation growing in the tidal flats.

Northern sea lions forage shallow waters and estuaries all along the British Columbia coast. The huge mammals are most readily observed at their breeding rookeries and haulout areas (rocky islets where they congregate to rest, socialize, and sun bathe). A few haulout sites are easily accessible for viewing the animals: Race Rocks is a short boat trip from Victoria, Active Pass is on the ferry route from Vancouver to Victoria, and Pachena Point is a half day's hike from the fishing village of Bamfield on the west coast of Vancouver Island.

Mature bulls, weighing a tonne or more, dominate the breeding rookeries. During June and July each gathers a harem of up to 30 females, forsaking food completely for the more urgent task of breeding. Females may move from harem to harem to increase their chances of conceiving. The following spring they are ready to mate again, only a week after giving birth to a single pup.

Northern sea lions are opportunistic feeders, taking squid, octopus, and locally abundant fish species such as rockfish, skate, salmon, halibut, and black cod. These habits incur the ire of fishermen. With the encouragement of a government bounty, thousands of sea lions have been slaughtered on the haulouts and rookeries. Occasionally, a bullet-ridden carcass washes ashore on British Columbia's beaches. Today only 25 percent of the original population remains.

OPPOSITE: Largest of the eared seals, northern sea lions laze on Anthony Island in the Queen Charlotte Islands.

RIGHT: Goose-necked barnacles fasten themselves to rocks in the intertidal zone. Their tough, elastic stalks bend back and forth with the surf.

Black oystercatchers are uncommon but permanent resident birds of the Pacific coast. Also known as redbills, these flamboyant, crow-sized shorebirds are easily recognized by their flattened, scarlet-coloured bill; bulging, yellow eyes; and pink legs. Contrary to their name, black oystercatchers eat few if any oysters. Feeding almost exclusively in the intertidal zone, they use their long bills to pry limpets from rocks, probe mussels, and pummel small crabs. At high tide when feeding areas are flooded, oystercatchers rest among the dark rocks where they are well camouflaged.

Like other shorebirds, oystercatchers are ground nesters. After a period of dramatic courtship and territorial demonstrations involving mutual bowing, flying chases, and whistle calls, two or three spotted, buff coloured eggs are laid in the hollow of a rocky islet or on an elevated beach in May or June. Both sexes incubate the eggs, and one month after hatching, the chicks can fly and open shellfish with their bills.

TOP: A bed of blue mussels is being attacked by snail-like whelks. The carnivorous whelk drills a hole through the mussel's shell, inserts its proboscis, and tears out the soft body of the mussel.

BOTTOM: Once plentiful in British Columbia waters, the sea otter was hunted to near extinction for its luxurious pelt. To aerate its coat for insulation from the cold waters of the Pacific, it grooms almost continually.

OPPOSITE: A black oystercatcher prepares to swallow a freshly shucked mussel.

Many types of molluscs inhabit the intertidal zone—clams, oysters, mussels, and snails. Anchored to the rocks by silky threads, one species of mollusc, the blue mussel, is gently rounded and knife-edged on one side to resist wave action. Water enters and exits the open shell through two siphons, while planktonic organisms are filtered out by the gills. However, the filtration process is indiscriminate—many shellfish are poisoned by industrial and agricultural wastes and even natural sea toxins such as red tide. Like other molluscs, blue mussels synthesize the abundant plankton of the ocean into a form that can be exploited by higher animals including humans.

Crustaceans are represented along the shoreline by many species. One of these, the acorn barnacle, is quite similar in the larval state to its relatives, the crabs and shrimps. However, after a period of growth, the larva fastens onto a hard surface, such as a rock or whale, never to move again. Lying on its back, it secretes a lime material that hardens into rock-hard plates. When the tide is out, the plates slide together to keep the animal moist and protected. With the return of the sea the top hatch opens and the barnacle's legs, now modified into feathers, extend into the swirl of plankton to feed.

OPPOSITE LEFT: Gulls carry clams aloft and bomb them onto rocks, breaking open the shells to expose the nourishing innards.

OPPOSITE TOP RIGHT: Acorn barnacles and rockweed adorn a rock. When the tide comes in, hatches on the barnacle's shell open, and a group of feathery plumes emerges to sweep the water for microscopic food.

OPPOSITE BOTTOM RIGHT: A hermit crab emerges cautiously from its appropriated moon snail shell. Its large, armoured front claws block the entrance should a predator threaten.

TOP RIGHT: The blood star ranges from the intertidal zone to depths of 650 metres. Its young are retained in brood pouches around the mouth.

BOTTOM RIGHT: A tidal pool is a rich environs for a great variety of marine plants and animals. Shown among the seaweeds are blue mussels, acorn barnacles, purple shore crabs, limpets, and snails.

Although rare in the interior of the province, the river otter is one of the most common mammals found along the coast. These playful members of the weasel family are active both on land and in the water, frolicking and foraging with boundless energy.

River otters have luxurious, dense, waterproof coats and lithe, streamlined bodies with webbed feet. Strong swimmers, they propel themselves through the water by flexing their entire bodies. Their large lungs retain enough oxygen for them to remain under water for approximately five minutes, a distinct advantage when diving after fish or digging into a muddy river bottom for frogs or crayfish.

Despite their apparent awkwardness when out of the water, river otters can travel overland for several kilometres and are agile enough to outrun humans. The female houses her litter of two or three on dry ground in abandoned muskrat or beaver lodges and burrows. After the young have grown their waterproof coats, they are dragged into the water by their mother where they soon continue with the rough and tumble play. Sometimes whole families of otters will amuse themselves by sliding down a mud or grass bank, zestfully splashing into the water.

LEFT: A typical section of British Columbia's wild, rocky, mountainous shoreline in the Queen Charlotte Islands.

OPPOSITE: *From the vantage point of a large piece of driftwood, a river otter scans its tidal hunting grounds near Victoria.*

The coastline of British Columbia is dappled and dotted with hundreds of small islands. Of these only a few offer the right conditions for colonial nesting seabirds—an abundant marine food supply and a remote location away from predators and disturbance by man. Some of the most prolific nesting colonies are found on Triangle Island off Cape Scott at the northern tip of Vancouver Island, on Solander Island off western Vancouver Island, and on a number of small islands in the Moresby group at the southern end of the Queen Charlottes.

Individual sea birds are very specialized in the type of terrain that they select for nesting. The tufted puffin needs turfed slopes in which to excavate an underground burrow and to cache its eggs. The pelagic cormorant, a weak flyer, prefers a site with high, steep cliffs to facilitate aerial takeoff. They use one nest for several years, piling up seaweed, grasses, and miscellaneous debris until the mound is almost a metre high. British Columbia's one million Cassin's auklets, small dark relatives of the puffin, dig burrows among shrubby growths of salal which are needed to cushion clumsy landings.

LEFT: A double-crested cormorant takes flight. Common along the south coast, these marine birds hang out their wings to dry when roosting on a rock or floating log.

OPPOSITE: A powerful surf breaks over the coastline near Port Renfrew on Vancouver Island.

PRECEDING PAGES: The tufted puffin nests on remote offshore islands. It flies quickly but with little maneuverability.

PLANTS AND ANIMALS OF THE SHORELINE

PLANTS

Black lichen
Sea lettuce
Tar spot
Feather boa
Rockweed
Eel grass
Turkish towel
Sea sac
Coral seaweed
Sea palm
Bull kelp
Alaria

MAMMALS

Grey whale
Killer whale
Harbour porpoise
Dall's porpoise
Northern sea lion
California sea lion
Harbor seal
Sea otter
River otter
Raccoon
Black bear

BIRDS

Bald eagle
Great blue heron
Belted kingfisher
Greater yellowlegs
Black oystercatcher
Dunlin
Western sandpiper
Black turnstone
Surf bird
Surf scoter
Harlequin duck
Red-breasted merganser
White-winged scoter
Western grebe
Pelagic cormorant
Double-crested
  cormorant
Pigeon guillemot
Tufted puffin
Common murre
Marbled murrelet
Cassin's auklet
Glaucous-winged gull
Western gull
Bonaparte's gull

FISH

Tidepool sculpin
Sand sole
Northern clingfish
High cockscomb
Penpoint gunnel
Salmon

MOLLUSCS

Mossy chiton
Fingered limpet
Purple olive snail
Japanese oyster
Horse clam
Heart cockle
Blue mussel
Rock scallop
Channeled whelk
Northern abalone
Pacific octopus

OTHER INVERTEBRATES

Acorn barnacle
Goosenecked barnacle
Broken back shrimp
Hermit crab
Purple shore crab
Purple seastar
Blood star
Sand dollar
Red sea urchin
Green sea urchin
Calcareous tube worm
Orange sea cucumber
Opalescent nudibranch
Aggregate anemone
Moon jellyfish
Sand hopper
Sand flea

OPPOSITE: Large flocks of sandpipers migrate along the coast, feeding along sandbars and mudflats exposed by the tides.

LEFT: The calm waters of Boundary Bay mark the southern limit of the mainland coast. During the winter the area is a haven for waterfowl, shorebirds, and many kinds of raptors including snowy owls.

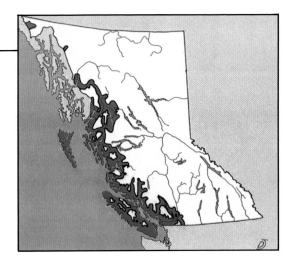

CHAPTER 2

THE COAST FORESTS

British Columbia's coast forest grows at low and middle elevations up to about 800 metres the length of the coastline, extending inland as much as 150 kilometres along major river valleys. It covers most of Vancouver Island and the Queen Charlotte Islands. Two types of forest are predominant. Drier regions in the rain shadow of the Olympic and Vancouver Island mountains are covered with open, park-like woodlands. However, most of the coast forest zone receives high amounts of precipitation and is overgrown with temperate rain forests renowned for their luxuriant vegetation and ancient trees of legendary proportions.

Temperate Rain Forest

On Meares Island near Tofino grows a western red cedar so huge that the average person requires more than 20 seconds just to walk around it. Soaring upward for more than 70 metres, the tree is so tall that generally it is one half a degree colder in the canopy than it is at ground level. Today most of British Columbia's giant trees have been sawed up and made into buildings, but at one time much of the province's coastal region was covered with virgin rain forests of awesome proportions. The best known remnants of the original forests can be found in Cathedral Grove, the Nimpkish Valley, and Pacific Rim National Park on Vancouver Island and in the South Moresby region of the Queen Charlottes. The abundant rainfall (up to four metres in one year), balmy temperatures (over 200 frost free days per year), and rich soils are the primary factors behind this incredible growth.

Four trees dominate the rain forest community: western red cedar, western hemlock, amabilis fir, and Sitka spruce. Easily recognized by its graceful, sweeping boughs and loose, ribbonous bark, the western red cedar withstands high winds and fire, living more than ten centuries in the case of some of British Columbia's oldest representatives. A more prevalent member of this forest community is the western hemlock, identified by its drooping tip. Its widespread abundance is due to the ability of its seedlings to grow quickly in the shade of the canopy. Sharing prominency with the western hemlock in wetter areas, and even more shade tolerant, is the amabilis fir. Although smaller than the western red cedar, both these trees reach colossal heights. Guarding the shoreline fringe along most of the coast is the Sitka spruce. It ranks with the Douglas-fir and western red cedar as one of the province's largest trees. Extremely tolerant of salt spray and soggy soil, it can grow to a height of 65 metres in only 100 years. Douglas-fir occurs throughout much of the rain forest, especially in drier regions in the south where it becomes dominant.

Along streams, riverbeds, and in open forests thrive several deciduous species—red alder, big-leaf maple, and Pacific dogwood. Big-leaf maple, the largest of these, bears leaves more than a foot wide. Early invaders of areas cleared by logging or fire, big-leaf maple and red alder brighten the usually sombre rain forest terrain in the autumn when their leaves turn gold. Pacific dogwood, the province's unofficial floral emblem, adds its colour to the forest in springtime when its showy, white blooms appear.

Surviving in the understorey of these forests are plants adapted to the low light levels that result from the dense canopy above. The floor is cluttered with deadfalls—branches broken off by ocean gales and immense, prostrate trunks toppled by disease. Sometimes entire root systems are torn out of the soil as the trees fall, creating in an instant towering, humped walls of earth and tangled roots. The debris begins to decompose quickly in the warm, wet climate, adding its nutrients to the already thick humus layer of the forest floor. Fungi sprout from the rotting wood, lichens drape the branches, and carpets of thick moss grow everywhere. There are delicate flowers and tall, elegant sword ferns. Where more sunlight filters through the canopy, salal, devil's club, and salmonberry bushes form barriers of prickly, impenetrable vegetation.

Dry Coastal Woodlands

In contrast to the lush rain forest is an open, grass-patched woodland on southeastern Vancouver Island and the Gulf Islands. It occupies the province's most westerly dry belt, receiving only 75 centimetres of rain a year. Once dominated by stands of large Douglas-fir, most of the landscape has been taken over by sleepy farms, scattered factories, sprawling suburbs, highways, and busy cities. Douglas-fir thrives in the rare pockets of native vegetation that remain. Growing in association with it are several unique tree species. Attaining a height of 25 metres, the arbutus has smooth, curving limbs and peeling, copper-red bark. It is Canada's only broad-leaved evergreen tree, keeping its foliage through the winter. Frequently associated with the arbutus is the Garry oak. A gnarled, twisted tree, it is British Columbia's only native oak. Growing best on level, dry terrain, its habitat has been severely depleted by human encroachment, and it is becoming increasingly rare.

These coastal woodlands are renowned for the display of wildflowers that takes place during the spring before the onset of the summer dry season. Exquisite tapestries of colour blanket the woodland openings and grassy knolls. Meadows are washed a startling royal blue by the blooms of camas. Shooting stars and satin-flowers shimmer in sunny glades, white fawn lilies carpet great stretches of the forest floor, and tucked into rocky crevices are yellow monkey flowers, blue-eyed Mary, and sea blush. The most common shrub of the woodland understorey, Oregon grape, has clusters of lemon coloured blooms.

Wildlife

Cut off from the mainland by the formidable barrier of the Coast Mountains, many animals of the coast forest region have evolved in isolation from their continental relatives and today are represented by distinctive subspecies. Columbian blacktail deer are smaller versions of the mule deer found away from the coast. Well adapted to coastal life, they do not hesitate to swim across saltwater straits to reach better forage. Coastal black bears, especially those on Vancouver Island and the Queen Charlottes, are larger than their inland cousins, perhaps owing to the gentler climate, abundant food, and lack of competition from grizzly bears. The two coastal subspecies of marten (an arboreal weasel that preys on small rodents on the forest floor) have fur more deeply coloured and less luxuriant than continental relatives. These differences are adaptations to the darker, warmer coast forest environment which allow them to stay cool and inconspicuous when hunting.

These dense forests are attractive habitats for bird watchers. The close vegetation limits visibility and makes sightings less frequent but all the more challenging. The songs of the winter wren and varied thrush enliven the underbrush, and the treetops twitch and resound with pileated woodpeckers, white-breasted nuthatches, western flycatchers, and chestnut-backed chickadees. The bubbling, clear song of the water-loving dipper can be heard along streamsides at any time of year.

PAGE 52: A moss-draped rain forest of Sitka spruce on the Queen Charlotte Islands.

RIGHT: The California poppy is an introduced wildflower which grows in the dry coastal woodlands of southern Vancouver Island and the Gulf Islands.

Surviving in great numbers, the black bear ranges throughout British Columbia. Its continued success is based on its adaptability to varied vegetative zones.

Although the black bear's diet is over 75 percent vegetable matter, it will eat almost anything. These opportunistic feeders dig for insect grubs and worms, hunt mice and other small mammals, fish for salmon, and eat carrion. They even climb trees to reach tender twigs, buds, and fruits and venture into subalpine meadows to feast on blueberries and huckleberries. Although bears usually feed at dawn and dusk, during the last weeks of summer they eat continuously. By autumn some have almost doubled their size, gaining as much as 14 kilograms per week. All this feeding is not without reason. Bears must accumulate sufficient fat during the summer to sustain them through a long winter of hibernation, which may last six months in cold regions of the province. With the first snowfall, they seek out a cave, hollow log, or rock crevice as their winter den.

Black bears are aggressively territorial. An adult male may share its home range with several mature females, but invasions by young bears or other mature males are usually met with savage attacks. Cubs are especially susceptible to serious injury, and, at the slightest sign of danger, the sow issues a hoarse snort that sends them scrambling up the nearest tree.

A black bear sow coaxes her cub down from a deadfall in the coastal forest near Winter Harbour on Vancouver Island. Very young bears cry when frightened and hum when contented.

Due to their high commercial value, most of the province's magnificent stands of virgin Douglas-fir were logged during the last century. The most massive tree still standing is the Red Creek Fir, located near Port Renfrew on Vancouver Island. It is probably Canada's largest tree, reaching a height of 80 metres and a circumference of almost 15 metres. During its long lifetime it has used more energy simply lifting water to its upper branches than it would take to raise four British Columbia jumbo ferries to the top of the Empire State Building. Even taller Douglas-firs grow in the remote Nimpkish Valley of northern Vancouver Island.

Impressive as these Douglas-firs may appear, they are only temporary, sub-climax species in the rain forest. Douglas-fir seedlings cannot grow in the shade of their parent trees and are eventually replaced by western hemlock, amabilis fir, or western red cedar—climax species which require less light for continued propagation. However, regular forest fire occurrence since the last glacial invasion 10,000 years ago has created enough open landscape for the Douglas-fir to retain its widespread status.

LEFT: A cougar lurks in the shadows of a western red cedar. These large, secretive cats prey on Columbian blacktail deer.

OPPOSITE: A relic stand of giant Douglas-fir and western hemlock at Cathedral Grove on Vancouver Island.

FOLLOWING PAGES: Red alder is a widespread, deciduous tree that quickly takes over areas cleared by fire or logging.

The red squirrel is found throughout British Columbia except for the Coast Range in the southern third of the province. An acrobatic member of the rodent family, it scampers head first up and down tree trunks, leaps spread-eagled from branch to branch, and even drops tens of metres to other trees.

Due to its high activity level, the red squirrel is more carnivorous than other squirrels, taking bird eggs, nestlings, and insects. Conifer cones, however, are the mainstay of its diet. With great energy and seemingly frenzied purpose, the red squirrel may cut virtually every cone from the branches within its territory. The cones are gathered in huge piles, or middens, that may be a metre deep and several metres across. One squirrel may gather as many as 14,000 cones by the end of a summer. Squirrels also hang fungi among tree branches to dry out and later store them along with berries and seeds in protected underground caches and tree cavities.

A red squirrel's home range is usually large enough to satisfy its food requirements. It protects this territory against intrusion from other squirrels with a varied repertoire of vocalizations, as well as stamping its feet, flicking its tail, and, if necessary, charging and chasing.

OPPOSITE: A red squirrel feeds on wild rose hips which have softened, blackened, and become more palatable after a winter of aging.

RIGHT: The leaves of a big-leaf maple can grow to more than a foot in width. In the summer the leaves of a large deciduous tree have the cooling effect of 20 room-size air conditioners.

The moist, shaded floor of an undisturbed coast forest is strewn with a jumble of rotting trunks, dead branches, seeds, cones, berries, and fallen leaves. A variety of snails and slugs tunnel through this chaotic rubble, feeding on fungi, decaying fruits, and dung. The most impressive feature of a snail is its spiral shell which it manufactures from calcium, carbon, and oxygen extracted from its food. If the surrounding environment is too dry, snails retreat into their shells until enough moisture returns to the air. Land snails are most active after dark when they cruise over the forest floor with the aid of a large, rippling, muscular foot.

Another interesting denizen of the forest understorey is the wolf spider. Its dark, mottled colours camouflage it among forest litter and debris. These shy hunters usually feed on insects which they locate by their well-developed senses of touch and vision. The numerous hairs on their long legs are also sensitive to vibration, air movement, and sound. Once the prey is located, it is either paralyzed or killed with poison injected from the spider's fangs.

LEFT: Stalked eyes and feelers guide the Pacific land snail on its search for algae and other plant material.

OPPOSITE: The wolf spider makes its home in the heavy, ridged bark of coastal trees.

The flora of the rain forest is adapted to shade and abundant precipitation. To maximize use of the little sunlight that filters through the thick, evergreen canopy, many flowering plants are broad-leaved and deep green from an abundance of chlorophyll, the catalyst of photosynthesis. Some shrubs, like salal, have thick, leathery leaves and stems to withstand heavy rains and snow that would otherwise flatten them to the ground. Others, like salmonberry, form tall thickets, reaching up for as much sunlight as possible. Few wildflowers grow in the deep shade of the forest floor. The heavily scented, glowing white, pastel blooms of single delight succeed in attracting insect pollinators despite the dim light.

The forest floor is frequently cluttered with the rotting trunks of fallen trees. Many of these deadfalls become nurselogs, providing a nutrient-rich, growing site for mosses, ferns, flowers, shrubs, and even trees. Although hundreds of tree seedlings may sprout on a nurselog, only a few actually survive and grow into young saplings. These young trees send their groping roots around the log and into the soil below. After several centuries the nurselog rots away completely, leaving behind the row of trees that it nurtured.

RIGHT: The trunks of fallen trees provide a rich habitat for seedlings.

OPPOSITE TOP LEFT: Single delight is a common wildflower of the rain forest.

OPPOSITE BOTTOM LEFT: A variety of fungi live off the dead and decaying matter of the rain forest.

OPPOSITE TOP RIGHT: The magenta flowers of salmonberry appear as early as March.

OPPOSITE BOTTOM RIGHT: Salal blooms with pink, urn-shaped flowers.

The Pacific tree frog ranges throughout most of southern British Columbia. This tiny amphibian, no larger than a human thumb, is superbly adapted to arboreal life. Camouflaged to surrounding vegetation, the body colour of individuals varies from green to brown or grey. Aided by long, slender legs and large, sticky toe pads, it can climb up almost any surface, sometimes venturing high into the canopy to feed on insects.

In early spring tree frogs congregate in open ponds, lakes, and swamps to breed. Females are attracted by the noisy mating chorus of the males, which fills the evening air for several weeks. Clusters of 500 or more eggs are laid. The male fertilizes them externally, clasping the female behind the forelimbs. In one to five weeks the tadpoles emerge. By late summer they have completed the process of metamorphosis, losing their tails and gills, developing limbs and lungs, and restructuring their digestive system to accommodate the carnivorous diet of adult frogs.

RIGHT: *Aided by sticky toe pads, a Pacific tree frog clings to dew-covered grass.*

OPPOSITE: *Black cottonwood leaves add a touch of colour to the coast forest in fall. Like other deciduous species, the black cottonwood grows in forest openings and along watercourses.*

In British Columbia the Garry oak is generally confined to the mild regions of southeastern Vancouver Island and the adjacent Gulf Islands. It grows slowly on dry, rocky knolls—a twisted, silvery silhouette of gnarled limbs topped by a shaggy crown of lobed, pebbly leaves. In the fall Garry oaks produce acorns that are eaten by a variety of birds and mammals. Squirrels and other rodents store the acorns for winter use while deer browse the foliage and twigs. In addition to their food value, oaks provide wildlife cover, and their leaves and twigs are used by many birds as nesting material.

Although primarily a bird of the American southwest, the band-tailed pigeon ranges as far north as British Columbia. Here it feasts on the wild harvest of the southern coast forest, relishing the fruits of elderberry, cascara, arbutus, and particularly Garry oak. As many as 50 acorns have been found in the crop of a single bird. Band-tails are distinguished by a narrow white band across the back of the neck and by their yellow bill. If approached too closely, these shy, forest birds take off with a loud flapping and fluttering of wings.

RIGHT: *Larger than domestic pigeons, band-tailed pigeons vocalize frequently with a deep, owl-like whoo-hoo.*

OPPOSITE: *Garry oak is one of the principal trees of the dry woodlands of southern Vancouver Island. Due to habitat reduction, it is becoming increasingly rare.*

Each spring the dry coastal woodlands abound with spectacular displays of wild flowering plants. Indian plum with its drooping clusters of white flowers is the first to bloom, quickly followed by another shrub, red-flowered currant. As the deciduous trees begin to unfurl their leaves, a profusion of delicate wildflowers pops up to make the most of the spring sunshine. Many are perennials fueling initial growth with energy stored in underground stems. Most are festooned with brightly coloured blooms designed to attract insect pollinators. Some, like satin-flower, only bloom a day or two before withering.

The arbutus, or Pacific madrone, lends a tropical flavour to the woodlands, with its peeling, lime-green bark and red trunk. In sheltered locations near the sea, it may bloom as early as March, exploding with clusters of creamy-white blossoms. By late summer the flowers have developed into masses of small, orange-red berries which are relished by many songbirds. The arbutus is Canada's only broad-leaved evergreen, keeping its thick, glossy leaves throughout the winter.

OPPOSITE: The peeling, reddish bark and twisted limbs distinguish the arbutus from its dry coastal woodland associate, the Douglas-fir.

RIGHT: The satin-flower is one of many spring wildflowers of open woodlands.

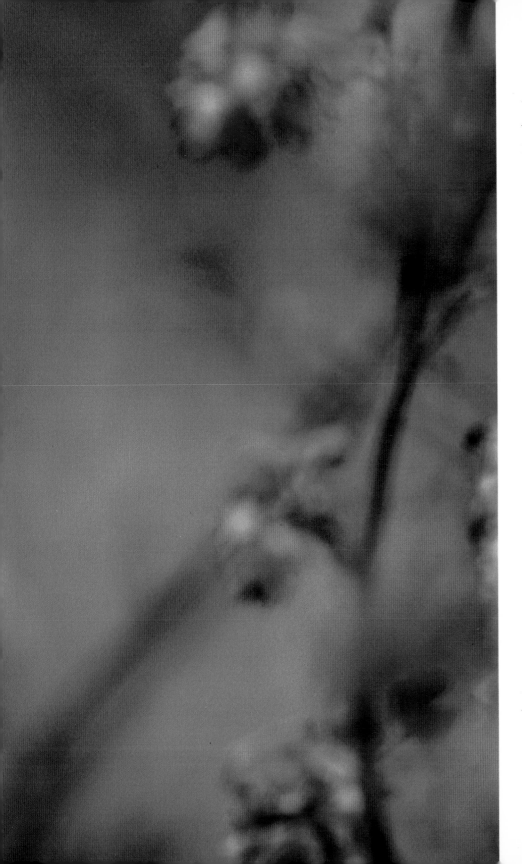

Every spring the coastal forests and woodlands are brightened by the tiny rufous hummingbird returning from its wintering grounds in Mexico. With dazzling speed and flashes of fiery iridescence, it jets about the glades and pathways in search of gnats, flies, spiders, and wildflowers. It is able to fly forward, backward, sideways, straight up and down, hover perfectly motionless, and accelerate and decelerate with incredible abruptness. No flier is more spectacular than the male hummingbird when it is excited and performing for a female.

Not much bigger than the end segment of a human thumb, the rufous hummingbird has one of the highest metabolic rates of any warm-blooded animal. A human expending energy at the same rate would require the evaporation of about 40 litres of perspiration per hour just to keep the skin temperature below the boiling point. The hummingbird must feed almost continually to avoid starvation. When the weather cools unexpectedly or food is scarce, it lowers its metabolism and rests in an unconscious, dormant state to conserve energy.

After feeding on the nectar of red-flowered currant, a rufous hummingbird flicks out its tongue to collect any excess. The appearance of this tiny bird in the spring coincides with the blooming of the red-flowered currant. With a high metabolism and heart rate of over 500 beats per minute, the rufous hummingbird eats almost continuously when active.

The flowers illustrated here represent only a small sample of the numerous species found during the spring in the dry coastal woodland habitat of Vancouver Island and the Gulf Islands. In Canada this region receives just fame for its early floral display. Local botanists list more than 25 species that bloom here in January alone.

TOP RIGHT: Blue-eyed Mary blooms in April and May on the coast where it is usually found in exposed, sunny areas of the forest.

BOTTOM RIGHT: Typically a roadside flower throughout the province, yarrow grows on dry, rock outcrops on southern Vancouver Island.

OPPOSITE LEFT: On the coast, Indian plum is the first shrub to herald the returning of spring, its tiny clusters of white flowers appearing in March.

OPPOSITE RIGHT: The range of the blue camas coincides closely with the distribution of the dry coastal woodlands.

PLANTS OF THE COAST FORESTS

TREES	SHRUBS/FERNS	WILDFLOWERS

Temperate Rain Forest

Western hemlock	Salal	Pipsissewa
Western red cedar	Salmonberry	Single delight
Amabilis fir	Devil's club	Starflower
Sitka spruce	Thimbleberry	Bunchberry
Douglas-fir	Low Oregon grape	Vanilla leaf
Yellow cedar	Red elderberry	Bleeding heart
Grand fir	Red huckleberry	Wild ginger
Big-leaf maple	Orange honeysuckle	Queen's cup
Red alder	Kinnikinnick	Fairy bells
Black cottonwood	Black twinberry	Indian pipe
Pacific dogwood	Deer fern	
	Sword fern	

Dry Coastal Woodlands

Douglas-fir	Tall Oregon grape	Blue camas
Arbutus	Red-flowered currant	Death camas
Garry oak	Snowberry	White fawn lily
Pacific dogwood	Ocean spray	Chocolate lily
Red alder	Indian plum	Satin-flower
Lodgepole pine	Evergreen huckleberry	Broad-leaved shooting star
	Manzanita	Blue-eyed Mary
	Licorice fern	Sea blush
		Yellow monkey flower
		Calypso orchid

ANIMALS OF THE COAST FORESTS

MAMMALS	BIRDS	OTHER ANIMALS
Columbian blacktail deer	Bald eagle	Pacific tree frog
Roosevelt elk	Band-tailed pigeon	Western garter snake
Black bear	Common raven	Alligator lizard
Cougar	Steller's jay	Rough skinned newt
Wolf	Pileated woodpecker	Northwestern salamander
Marten	Rufous-sided towhee	Banana slug
Raccoon	Varied thrush	Pacific land snail
Red squirrel	Townsend's warbler	
Douglas squirrel	Rufous hummingbird	
Deer mouse	Winter wren	

Columbian blacktail bucks crowned with velvet antlers retreat to the concealing safety of a thicket as the sun rises.

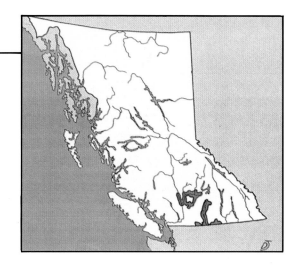

CHAPTER 3

THE GRASSLANDS

Much of the south-central area of British Columbia is covered by grassland and semi-desert. Guarded by mountain ranges that rob moisture from weather systems originating on the Pacific coast, these low-lying regions receive less than 40 centimetres of rain each year, not enough to support forest growth. Usually found at elevations of less than 1000 metres, these dry areas run in long strips along valley floors sandwiched between slopes overlain with evergreen forests. Most of this habitat occurs in two regions: the basins of the Chilcotin, Thompson, Nicola, and Fraser Rivers to the north and the Okanagan and Similkameen River systems to the south.

Before the arrival of white settlers, three-quarters of this open terrain was covered with bunchgrass—tough, dense, chest-high clumps about as thick as a man's leg. As a result of the sparse rainfall, the grass tufts were surrounded by areas of bare soil. Here and there the dull greens of sagebrush and the erect, hairy limbs of rabbitbush relieved the monotony of the ground cover.

Today, due to decades of overgrazing by domestic livestock, much of the native bunchgrass has been displaced by cheat grass, mustard, pasture sage, and sagebrush. In the south, as well as other areas, large-scale irrigation projects provide water for neatly cultivated orchards and vineyards, vastly altering the original habitat. Nevertheless, the area retains in many places a measure of its unique prairie character, the pungent aroma of sage and patchy turf harmonizing with the soft, grey-green hues of the sparse landscape.

Over a significant portion of these grasslands grow broad-leaved plants, many of which produce eye-catching blooms during the warmer seasons. Early spring is enlivened by the pink, ground hugging petals of bitterroot and the nodding, fragrant blooms of yellow fritillary. As summer approaches, the vivid colours of scarlet gilia, brown-eyed Susan, and numerous thistles adorn the open hillsides. Although the summer sun scorches out most of the colour, the terrain regains a measure of its gaiety in the fall when the foliage of sumac and poison ivy glows brilliant red.

A transition zone, sometimes quite extensive, occurs on the hillsides between the low-lying grasslands and the montane forests which take over at higher altitudes. This is a region of savannah—sunbaked, open terrain dominated by grasses with a regular scattering of trees, primarily ponderosa pine and Rocky Mountain juniper, but occasionally Douglas-fir. In May these hills are sprinkled unforgettably with the gold blooms of balsam root sunflower, a bold, flashing symbol of spring. Another unique attraction is squaw currant, a dense shrub festooned in the summer with bright red berries which are relished by many bird species.

In the open emptiness of the grasslands, wildlife is often visible and audible from afar. Western meadowlarks broadcast their flute-like calls, kingbirds swoop aggressively from dead branches to chase airborne insects, turkey vultures work quietly at mounds of carrion, while teams of chattering, black-billed magpies flutter about, impatient for a turn at the carcasses. The screams of red-tailed hawks float down from the blue, cloudless skies. The brushy cover bordering creeks and shady canyons is home for such exotic-sounding birds as the black-headed grosbeak, yellow-bellied sapsucker, and Canada's smallest bird, the calliope hummingbird, weighing in at less than half a dozen aspirins. Coyotes trot across the wastes, pausing often to peer over their shoulders. A few rock bluffs, steep canyons, and benchlands harbour California bighorn sheep, a species with a small and vulnerable population. Burly, low-slung badgers lounge around the grasses near the humped entrances to their dens, soaking up sun.

Semi-desert

The extreme south of this arid region is invaded for 50 kilometres along the Okanagan and Similkameen valleys by fingers of semi-desert habitat, part of an extensive desert region that stretches all the way to Mexico. Rainfall is less here than elsewhere in the province; summers are blistering hot, and winters are mild. Bunchgrass, sagebrush, and antelope bush, a stiff-limbed, scraggly shrub that reaches its northern limit here, comprise the dominant ground cover. Milkweed with its thick, hair-covered, moisture-retaining leaves grows in the driest regions. Another typical desert plant found here is prickly pear cactus; its fleshy, green lobes are armed with piercing, clinging spines and crowned by brilliant yellow flowers during early summer.

This environment supports a variety of animals adapted to cope with the dry climate and sparse landscape. Sage thrashers, canyon wrens, and rock wrens find suitable nesting sites in the rocky terrain, and their serenades echo through the canyons in spring. Rattlesnakes and alligator lizards move about the rock outcrops, controlling their body temperatures by moving in and out of the sun or shade. Spadefoot toads dig their way into the sand to escape the broiling sun. Crouched amidst the withered grasses are white-tailed jackrabbits equipped with antenna-like, heat radiating ears as long as a man's hand. Although a small region in terms of area, the unique plants and animals of this life zone add immeasurably to the natural diversity of the province.

PAGE 80: Ponderosa pine/bunchgrass habitat in the southern Okanagan Valley.

OPPOSITE: Bobcats favour the mixed cover of lower elevations found in the province's dry interior valleys.

The bottomlands of the dry interior harbour a rich flora and fauna. Shielded from the drying effects of sun and wind, these depressions accumulate enough moisture to promote the widespread growth of woody plants. Within these miniature forest environments live animals wholly adapted to forest life as well as grassland species seeking shelter.

These low-lying habitats are dominated by moisture-loving tree species like willow, cottonwood, and birch. The shade and wind shelter they create permit the growth of a varied understorey of shrubs and flowers. Elderberry, sumac, and red osier dogwood are common shrubs whose flowers and fruits punctuate the thickets with aroma and colour.

The forested bottomlands provide food, shelter, and reproductive sites for many birds and animals. Generally feeding by night in open terrain, mule deer and coyotes retreat to thickets for protection during the day. Red-tailed hawks nest in the treetops but hunt rodents on the grasslands. Other animals, like squirrels, porcupines, raccoons, woodpeckers, nuthatches, and chickadees, are more permanent residents of the wooded bottomlands.

OPPOSITE: Bottomlands and coulees collect moisture and provide shade and wind protection for a variety of trees and shrubs.

RIGHT: Lupines grow on the hillsides of the dry interior. More than 20 species of this wildflower are found in many differing habitats throughout the province.

The badger is superbly adapted to the grasslands of the dry interior. Its low-slung, burly frame is camouflaged by a sandy brown pelage that blends in with the dusty hues of the surrounding landscape. Equipped with stout forearms and long, curved claws, this giant, digging weasel is a powerful excavator that can burrow its way out of sight within a few minutes.

After sundown the badger ventures out of its underground home in search of large, burrowing rodents, particularly ground squirrels. Once its prey flees underground, the badger digs straight down, trapping the unsuspecting quarry in its burrow. Mice, voles, ground nesting birds and their eggs, and, on occasion, even rattlesnakes are part of the badger's fare.

Although generally solitary, the badger has developed a unique hunting relationship with the coyote. While a badger digs into a burrow, a coyote waits at one of its side entrances, ready to pounce on squirrels that try to escape. Sometimes both predators rush through a ground squirrel colony, creating such chaos with their two-pronged attack that the rodents become disoriented and are caught before they regain their senses and retreat underground.

RIGHT: The badger is a burrowing weasel that inhabits the grasslands of British Columbia's interior.

OPPOSITE: The monotony of the dry sagebrush flats near Ashcroft is relieved by a meandering stream and the plants it nourishes. Growing in the moist thicket are red osier dogwood, squaw currant, black cottonwood, white clematis, mountain alder, willow, Douglas maple, and black hawthorne.

The song sparrow breeds throughout most of British Columbia. It is represented by many subspecies, varying in colour from pale, sandy brown to a dark, charcoal shade. Generally, the plumage is brown above with heavy brown streaking and a prominent, central breast spot on the white underparts. In flight the song sparrow pumps or twitches its relatively long tail up and down.

Most of British Columbia's song sparrows winter south of the United States border. In the spring their powerful and melodious songs announce their return to the grasslands. The song of the male consists of a few long, mellow notes followed by a series of short notes and trills. Singing is part of the male's territorial and courtship behaviour and is accompanied by the fluffing and raising and lowering of one or both wings.

After mating the female builds a cup nest in the grasses or shrubbery. Usually, three to six green, speckled eggs are laid, and within a couple of weeks they hatch. The young leave the nest when they are only ten days old, usually before they can fly. Two clutches are often raised each year.

OPPOSITE: Sagebrush, juniper, and ponderosa pine cover the rocky hillsides of the Similkameen Valley.

LEFT: A song sparrow alights to sing its familiar courtship melody. Its display will attract females and announce its territorial claims to other males.

Many types of plants grow in association with the grasses of the dry interior. Wildflowers are found practically everywhere—along valley benches, in coulees, along fence rows, roadsides, and stream banks—adding tremendously to the diversity of the grasslands. Other grassland plants arrived with the early settlers as stray seeds in sacks of grain. Generally thought of as weeds, some, like thistles, clovers, and dandelions, are nevertheless beautiful and of value to wildlife. Their nectar feeds bees, flies, butterflies, moths, and other insects. Hoofed mammals, rodents, and hares browse on the leaves and stems. Predators, from spiders to cougars, in turn take nourishment from these herbivores.

OPPOSITE LEFT: Brown-eyed Susan blooms during the summer, its bright flowers attracting bees, butterflies, and other insects.

OPPOSITE TOP RIGHT: Camouflaged to its floral background, a crab spider waits in ambush for visiting insects.

OPPOSITE BOTTOM RIGHT: Forget-me-nots add a pale splash of blue to the moist fields and marshes of interior valley bottoms.

RIGHT: A giant swallowtail butterfly siphons nectar from a thistle.

The range of the western rattlesnake extends into the drier regions of south-central British Columbia. On each side of the rattler's head, between the eye and nostril, is a heat-sensitive depression, or pit, that enables it to locate warm-blooded prey in complete darkness. As the rattler opens its mouth to strike, a pair of curved, hollow fangs near the front of the upper jaw swing forward rapidly and inject venom into the victim. The venom is a complex mixture of proteins that acts primarily on the victim's red blood cells, destroying them and causing the breakdown of tissue.

These vipers also bear a distinctive rattle on their tail. It consists of a series of flattened, interlocking, dry, horny segments that buzz or rattle when shaken. A new segment is added each time the snake sheds its skin, normally two to four times a year.

The rattlesnake's activity is regulated by temperature. In the spring and fall it hunts during the day, taking mostly small mammals and birds. The heat of summer forces the snake to feed after dark on nocturnal rodents. Usually in September between four and eight young are born live.

OPPOSITE: Alarmed, a western rattlesnake coils up and samples air-borne scents with its flicking tongue.

TOP RIGHT: The western toad lives in burrows of its own making or those of small rodents.

BOTTOM RIGHT: A western painted turtle is fond of sun basking, and sometimes a dozen can be observed on a single floating log.

British Columbia contains approximately 70 percent of the world's population of the endangered California bighorn sheep. They are confined to the dry, rocky terrain of the province's interior. The largest herd consists of 1,000 sheep and occupies 5,000 hectares between the Fraser and Chilcotin Rivers. Here the grassy benchlands offer good grazing, and the precipitous river canyons provide refuge from predators.

Bighorn sheep live in small, sexually segregated bands. Led by older females, the maternal bands consist of ewes, lambs, and immature rams. They feed and migrate separately from the older rams which form their own groups. During the summer all the sheep are on the move, searching for good grazing and visiting salt licks. While feeding in open terrain, the herding behaviour gives added protection from predators like mountain lions, wolves, and bobcats.

During the autumn rut the breeding males join the maternal bands. Charging and head-smacking duels between rival males are common. Spectacular clashes sometimes result in the massive, curled horns breaking off. These displays determine dominance between males and subsequent access to females. Receptive ewes generally mate with several different rams during the same rut. In late May a single lamb or occasionally, twins are born.

RIGHT: Growing along a sandy wash-out near Osoyoos, the yellow flowers of rabbitbush are buffeted by the wind. The mass of blooms appears in August and September.

OPPOSITE: Scattered bands of California bighorn sheep roam the valleys and canyons of the interior.

The coyote, song dog of the prairie, is best known for its nighttime serenades. Its plaintive calls consist of a quick series of yelps followed by a falsetto howl. Found throughout British Columbia, coyotes are most numerous in the grasslands where they are south of the range of their chief predator, the wolf.

Although this slim, buff coloured carnivore will eat almost anything it can hunt down, nearly 90 percent of its diet consists of rabbits, hares, mice, ground squirrels, and carrion. Agile and swift, it can chase down prey at speeds up to 65 kilometres per hour. Although coyotes sometimes hunt in packs, pairs are more common in the grasslands.

Coyotes mate in early spring. After a gestation period of 60 days, the pups, usually six in number, are born. The young, which are cared for by both mother and father, leave the underground den and begin roaming with their parents approximately two months after birth.

OPPOSITE: The coyote prefers the dry parklands, grasslands, and desert habitats of the interior.

TOP RIGHT: Abundant before the rise of agriculture, the white-tailed jackrabbit inhabits the sagebrush plains of the Okanagan Valley in greatly reduced numbers. It can sprint up to 70 kilometres per hour in five metre leaps.

BOTTOM RIGHT: A burrowing owl regurgitates a pellet outside its subterranean nesting site. The pellet is a compacted ball of rodent bones and fur and insect exoskeletons—the undigested leftovers of the owl's victims. Government and private organizations are trying to re-establish the rare burrowing owl as a breeding species within the province.

Few plants are as hardy or as well adapted to survival as the many species of grasses found in British Columbia. Grass can be trampled, chewed off to the ground, frozen, drowned, desiccated, or burnt and yet survive to thrive anew once better conditions return. Self-pollinating, grass needs only a breath of wind to start the process of seed production. Once developed, these tough seeds are equipped with kite-like appendages which transport them on the wind, or they may have hooks that snag on a passing mule deer or bighorn sheep.

The roots are perhaps the most amazing of all. Branching out horizontally, they are able to send up new stems. During the summer dry season, the microscopic root hairs can probe the soil to take in the most infinitesimal bits of moisture. The roots of some species grow to depths of three metres and the total system, including the many small branches and root hairs, can be over 500 kilometres long.

OPPOSITE LEFT: The spiny, fleshy clumps of prickly pear cactus bear tissuey, yellow blooms during June and July.

OPPOSITE TOP RIGHT: The sage thrasher sings in rich, musical phrases from atop a rocky outcrop or a clump of rabbitbush.

OPPOSITE BOTTOM RIGHT: A western tailed blue butterfly perches momentarily on the three-toothed leaves of sagebrush.

RIGHT: The rains and snowmelt of spring create a profuse growth of wildflowers and grasses in the semi-desert regions near Osoyoos.

Cedar waxwings breed throughout most of south-central British Columbia. These smooth, sculptured songbirds exhibit a prominent crest, distinctive black mask, pale greenish-yellow belly, and yellow-tipped tail. Waxwings derive their name from the bright red, wax-like drops that form on the tips of the adults' secondary wing and tail feathers. The function of these droplets, which are a prolongation of the feather shafts, is unknown.

Like other waxwings, this species eats many kinds of wild fruits. Large flocks of waxwings feed close together, sometimes gorging themselves until they are almost unable to fly. During the spring and summer they revert to fly catching, darting from perches to catch high protein snacks in mid-air.

In early summer three to five pale grey or blue-grey, spotted eggs are laid in a bulky nest made of twigs, bark strips, plant fibre, and rootlets. After approximately two weeks of incubation by the female, the eggs hatch. The very young chicks are fed insects, but within a few days fruits are added to their diet. About 14-18 days after hatching, the young leave the nest. Usually, one and sometimes two broods are raised a season.

RIGHT: Larger watercourses in the interior grasslands support the growth of varied trees and shrubs.

OPPOSITE: A cedar waxwing forages on the red berries of squaw currant near Vaseux Lake. This compact shrub grows at the foot of dry slopes or along barren river benches.

PLANTS AND ANIMALS OF THE GRASSLANDS

TREES

Ponderosa pine
Douglas-fir
Rocky mountain juniper
Water birch
Western choke cherry
Trembling aspen

SHRUBS/FERNS

Sagebrush
Rabbitbush
Antelope bush
Squaw currant
Mock orange
Blue elderberry
Smooth sumac
White clematis
Soopolallie
Woodsia fern

WILDFLOWERS

Yellow fritillary
Bitterroot
Prickly pear cactus
Purple aster
Scarlet gilia
Balsam root sunflower
Evening primrose
Brown-eyed Susan
Yarrow
Desert lupine
Gumweed

MAMMALS

California bighorn sheep
Mule deer
White-tailed deer
Bobcat
Coyote
Badger
White-tailed jackrabbit
Pocket gopher
Pocket mouse

BIRDS

Red-tailed hawk
Golden eagle
Turkey vulture
Burrowing owl
Black-billed magpie
Western meadowlark
Bobolink
Mountain bluebird
Western kingbird
Sage thrasher
Brewer's sparrow
Rock wren
Calliope hummingbird

OTHER ANIMALS

Western rattlesnake
Bull snake
Western toad
Spadefoot toad
Leopard frog
Western painted turtle

LEFT: Treed hillsides provide daytime cover for deer which venture out after dark to feed on the grasslands.

OPPOSITE: In British Columbia, white-tailed deer generally inhabit thickets along the Columbia and Kootenay River systems.

CHAPTER 4

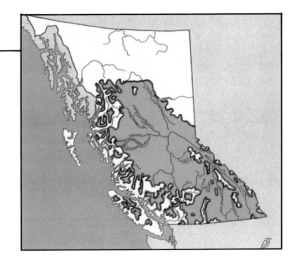

THE INTERIOR FORESTS

The British Columbia interior is blanketed by forests seemingly endless in extent and quite variable in biotic make-up. In general the character of these forests is a product of rainfall, elevation, temperature, and soil type. As elsewhere in the province, the homogeneity of the vegetation communities is disrupted by localized topographic and climatic peculiarities and the presence of streams, rivers, and lakes.

Columbian Forest

When moist air masses originating in the Pacific Ocean pass over the high terrain of the Columbia Mountains some 300 kilometres inland they release considerable precipitation, in the process creating an extensive vegetation zone not unlike the lush rainforest of the coast. These forests occupy the lower slopes and valleys of the Columbia Mountains. A similar, but smaller, wet forest zone is found further north along the Nass and Skeena River systems.

With the exception of Sitka spruce, the major coastal trees are found here as characteristic species—the valleys are crowded with solid, formidable towers of western red cedar, western hemlock, and interior Douglas-fir. Grand fir, western yew, western larch, and western white pine are also common. The understorey is luxuriant, resplendent with ferns and such varied shrubs as devil's club, black elderberry, and false azalea. It is decorated everywhere with thick wrappings of moss and dangling lichens. Rows of seedlings spring from the immense, soggy, rotting, fertile carcasses of downed trunks, and from a jumble of storm-broken limbs and branches sprout neon molds and arresting exhibits of erotically sculptured fungi. The forest floor grows wildflowers similar to those encountered in the coast forest. Golds of skunk cabbage set aglow the cedar bogs, tiny, whorled trumpets of blue-eyed Mary rise from mats of sun-exposed moss, and the snowy bracts of bunchberry carpet the forest openings.

Of the varied wildlife found in the Columbian forest the woodland caribou is the most distinctive and unique. A species left over from the Ice Age, here it is an oddity, surviving in a pocket far to the south of its native, boreal forest habitat. Well adapted for winter survival, the caribou is insulated by a thick coat of hollow hairs and equipped with large, flat hooves that assist travel through deep snow. The lichen gardens of the mature cedar and hemlock forests are its primary source of food, a supply that has been depleted by logging to the detriment of the caribou population.

Montane Forest

Spreading over the lower slopes and flats below the subalpine forests are the drier, sparser, montane forests. Differing considerably in vegetative make-up, they occupy highly variable terrain over a large area of the central interior region.

In the south much of the Okanagan, Similkameen, and Thompson valleys are taken up by grass-patched, sun-dappled stands of Douglas-fir and ponderosa pine. With its long, floppy, thickly bunched needles, its fissured, rusty orange bark, and its huge, ornamental cones littering the ground, the ponderosa pine imparts a festive aura to these bright, aromatic woodlands. Broken mats of brittle juniper and kinnikinnick make up the shrubbery of the understorey. During warm seasons the ground is asplash with wildflowers—lupines, brown-eyed Susans, daisies, and gumweed. Higher up the slopes western larch invades the community, displacing the pine and brightening the autumn landscape with the burnished gold of its needles. Bird life becomes very apparent in the openness of the southern pine woods. The soft cooing of mourning doves wafts through the glades; roadside wires are picketed with kestrels and western meadowlarks; small noisy flocks of pygmy nuthatches roam the treetops while overhead golden eagles wheel silently through the wind.

In the central and northern regions decreasing temperature and different soils cause changes in the montane forest vegetation. Douglas-fir is still present, but ponderosa pine is replaced by lodgepole pine north of the South Thompson River valley. In places the rolling hills are packed monotonously with its bare, stilt-like trunks. Clumps of trembling aspen encircle the marshes and cling to the banks of every stream and coulee. These forests are broken by numerous wet meadows, ponds, and lakes which support a rich community of birds and mammals. Ruddy ducks, mallards, canvasbacks, northern shovellers, teal, and American widgeon quack, whistle, chatter, and wail their courtship songs into the spring air. The underbrush is carved by the pathways of moose, wolf, deer, and bear while the openings are home for badgers and yellow-bellied marmots. Red squirrel, flying squirrel, fisher, and marten inhabit the forest's upper storey.

Subalpine Forest

Generally found at mountain elevations above 1200 metres from the Rockies to the Pacific coast inlets, the subalpine forests are comprised of species adapted to the fleeting growing seasons of brief summers and the deep, muffling snows of lingering winters. These forests mantle the mountain heights, in places their thin, ice-shedding, spire-like trees climbing near vertical slopes, clumping and growing stunted as they merge into the alpine tundra zone.

The subalpine forests are mostly coniferous, composed of Engelmann spruce, white spruce, and alpine fir with northern regions given over to expanses of lodgepole pine. In these relatively open stands the underbrush is thick with low growing shrubs such as mountain huckleberry, mountain ash, white rhododendron, twinberry, and kinnikinnick. Near timberline during the short spate of summer a dazzling collection of mountain wildflowers, buzzing with insect traffic, inundates the forest's openings. In the fall porcupines burden some treetops, feeding on tender bark and foliage, their mating wails echoing through the crisp, night air. These mountain forests are home to a host of other mammals as well—the varying hare, grizzly bear, red squirrel, and white-tailed and mule deer are but a few. Twittering flocks of small birds—pine siskins, redpolls, and red crossbills—wander the forests in winter, foraging the upper storey for cone seeds. They are shadowed by solitary predators, the northern shrike with its black mask and heavy, flesh-sheering bill, and the ever hungry, sparrow-sized pygmy owl.

PAGE 104: Forests of white spruce and lodgepole pine cover the elevated slopes along the Thompson River.

RIGHT: The largest and most powerful falcon in North America, a gyrfalcon tears at a ring-necked pheasant it has just killed. Birds of the northern tundra, gyrfalcons wander southward into British Columbia during the winter. They prey mainly on other large birds such as grouse, ptarmigan, pheasants, and ducks.

Fireweed, a member of the evening primrose family, is found across British Columbia. This unusually tall, pink flower springs up as temporary covering in areas cleared by fire or logging. In British Columbia where forest fires destroy thousands of hectares of timbered land every summer, and logging is an important industry, the beautiful blossoms of fireweed are a common sight. Fireweed is also a valuable honey plant, and bee keepers have been known to follow after logging camps to take advantage of the associated profusion of fireweed.

By late summer the flowers develop seed pods which split open, releasing hundreds of seeds with silky plumes. Small mammals, such as chipmunks and pikas, eat the seeds while large, hoofed browsers, like deer and elk, graze on the plants.

Ruffed grouse are noted for their unusual and distinctive courtship behaviour. Instead of singing, breeding males challenge rivals and attract females by rapidly beating their cupped wings in the air, producing a hollow-toned, drumming sound. The male's wing strokes are slow at first but increase to a rate of 20 strokes per second until the sound becomes a rapid whir. The drumming can be heard almost half a mile away. As part of the courtship display, the male also raises its spectacular ruff and crest and fans its tail feathers.

After mating, the hen scrapes a slight hollow at the base of a tree or log. To cushion her dozen or so eggs, she lines the well-camouflaged nest with a soft layer of leaves and molted feathers. Although the chicks can fly a week after hatching, they do not leave their protective mother until almost three months later.

OPPOSITE: Seeds of fireweed float over the expanse of Columbian and subalpine forest in the Arrow Lakes region.

TOP RIGHT: The rubber boa climbs into shrubbery to prey on small birds, mammals, and lizards. It inhabits moist environments in the interior.

BOTTOM RIGHT: The ruffed grouse is widespread throughout the province, inhabiting coniferous forests during winter and woodland openings in summer.

The American dipper is found near mountain streams throughout British Columbia. It is the only truly aquatic songbird in North America, exhibiting superb adaptations for living in or close to the water. A large preening gland, ten times the size of that of any other songbird, supplies oil to keep the feathers waterproof. Soft, filmy plumage and a thick undercoat of down insulate the dipper's body from the icy cold of mountain streams. Water is kept out of the bird's eyes by a nictitating membrane and from its nostrils by a movable flap.

The dipper feeds on a variety of aquatic life. A strong, underwater swimmer, it uses its wings to "fly" to depths of six metres to reach insects at the bottom of ponds or streams. It also feeds on aquatic worms and searches under rocks and stones for clams, snails, and fry.

During the spring the female builds an oven-shaped nest near water or sometimes under a waterfall. She lays four to five white eggs and incubates them for about two weeks. One month after hatching, the young can be seen perched along the edge of a stream, bobbing up and down as frequently as once a second in true dipper fashion.

OPPOSITE: Fed by the melting snow pack, Coffee Creek flows into Kootenay Lake in the Columbian forest.

LEFT: A species found along rivers and streams throughout much of the province, an American dipper pauses before plunging under water to forage on the bottom.

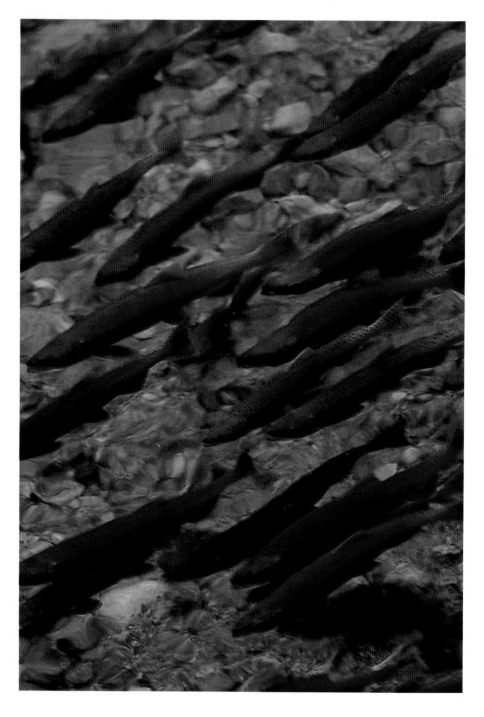

Five species of salmon inhabit British Columbia's waters: the chinook, pink, chum, coho, and sockeye. All species have similar habits. An oddity is the Kokanee salmon which is a land-locked sockeye found in many lakes in the province. Unlike coastal species which spend most of their life in the sea, land-locked salmon are totally confined to lakes and rivers.

For all salmon, life begins in the gravel bed of a freshwater stream or river. Newly hatched salmon are equipped with sac-like appendages that nourish them through their first few days of life. When the sacs are used up, the fry feed on insects and plankton for a few weeks. Coastal species then swim downstream to salt water, spending the next two to eight years foraging the Pacific Ocean. They often swim hundreds of kilometres from their birthplace but on reaching maturity, abandon their odyssey and begin a miraculous return journey to the very stream where they once were hatched. Here spawning occurs. The eggs are laid in a hollow excavated by the female's tail and then are fertilized externally by the male. All species die almost immediately after spawning, their exhausted bodies littering streams and attracting a host of scavengers—bears, gulls, eagles, and crows to name a few.

LEFT: Kokanee salmon turn scarlet and develop hooked jaws and large, fighting teeth during the spawning season.

OPPOSITE: A common raptor throughout the province, an osprey arrives at its nest site in the Creston Valley with a freshly caught catfish.

The deer mouse derives its name from its bi-coloured coat, rufous above and white below, which resembles the fur of a deer. This small rodent actually has three pelages during its lifetime: the juvenile coat is dark grey above and white below, the subadult coat is more brownish, and rufous tones appear in the adult's coat.

These herbivores eat the seeds of a wide variety of grasses and herbs as well as salmonberries, strawberries, raspberries, cherries, and dogwood fruits. It has been estimated that a deer mouse can consume between two and three hundred Douglas-fir seeds daily—bad news for foresters were it not for the fact that these mice feed on a number of insects and caterpillars injurious to trees.

Deer mice reproduce at a remarkable rate. One pair is theoretically capable of producing four generations a season, and if maximum size litters were to survive, the offspring would number 10,000 within one year. In the wild they usually produce two or three litters per year, with two to eight young per litter. Due to their abundance, deer mice are an important link in the forest's energy web, constituting a staple food for owls, weasels, and foxes.

OPPOSITE LEFT: The bracken fern is the most widespread fern in the province, occurring at lower elevations in coniferous forests.

OPPOSITE RIGHT: In the fall frost tinges the leaves of bunchberry a scarlet hue.

RIGHT: The deer mouse lives in almost any type of terrestrial habitat throughout the province.

During the summer growing season, subalpine animals are busy accumulating food to sustain them during the winter. Bears, marmots, and ground squirrels store the energy from plant matter within their bodies as fat. Black bears gain about ten kilograms of fat for every 100 kilograms of berries they consume. Chipmunks and pikas use a different strategy. Unable to build up fat reserves, they cache seeds, dried grasses, and other plant matter below ground.

To conserve energy during the winter, many animals enter a dormant state. During hibernation, a black bear's heart rate drops from 40 beats per minute to ten, and its respiration is cut by half. Waste liquids are cleansed and recycled within its body for up to three months to avoid heat loss through urination. The chipmunk, except for briefly visiting its food cache every four or five days, passes the winter curled up in a still, cold ball with its body temperature reduced to a few degrees above freezing, taking a breath only once or twice a minute. Despite such efficient methods of conserving energy, hibernating animals lose up to 40 percent of their weight by spring.

TOP RIGHT: Blueberries ripen by late summer in subalpine regions where they are a favoured food of black bears.

BOTTOM RIGHT: The creamy pink flowers of black mountain huckleberry develop into black berries by fall.

OPPOSITE: The black bear has amazingly flexible lips which are free from its gums. They can be manipulated with great dexterity, assisting the bear in eating small, slippery berries.

The least chipmunk is one of the many similar chipmunk species of British Columbia. Preferring areas of tangled brush, logs, and rocks, it is most common at higher reaches of the subalpine forests and above timberline. The least chipmunk appears above ground shortly after sunrise and spends the daylight hours in search of a variety of foods, zipping about the home territory to chase down a beetle, gather seeds, or feast on its favourite food—berries. As it forages, the chipmunk stuffs a considerable amount of material into its elastic cheek pouches, eventually carrying the booty back to its burrow to be eaten in safety or stored for later use.

Once winter sets in, the chipmunk is seldom seen. It spends most of its time in deep sleep, stirring only occasionally to grab a quick snack from one of its subterranean caches. As a small herbivore, the chipmunk is an important prey species for foxes, bobcats, weasels, hawks, owls, and snakes.

LEFT: Alpine fir and mountain hemlock near Idaho Lookout in the Selkirk Mountains.

OPPOSITE TOP LEFT: Yellow-bellied marmots inhabit dry, rocky uplands in the southern interior of the province. They burrow under massive boulders to prevent bears and badgers from digging them out.

OPPOSITE BOTTOM LEFT: The least chipmunk lives in rocky or broken terrain at middle elevations up to timberline.

OPPOSITE RIGHT: Subalpine forest in the Cascade Mountains near Hope.

Closely related species with similar habits, both mule deer and white-tailed deer are found in British Columbia. The white-tailed deer's most impressive feature is its big, flag-like tail that is almost a foot long. Brown above and white below, the deer flicks it from side to side or hoists it high when in flight, flashing the snowy undersurface. The billowy tail is a striking accent to the deer's trim outline, reddish-fawn coat, and white belly, throat, and eye ring. The antlers of the buck, formed by a single pair of main, forward-sweeping beams with minor tines, differ from the mule deer's multi-branched headgear.

Smell plays an important part in the life of the mule deer. It has specialized glands located between the lobes of its hooves that deposit scent with each step. These scent trails enable deer to keep track of each other's movements and also help does to find wandering fawns. Important in establishing dominance between animals are tufts of hair known as tarsal glands. They are located on the insides of the deer's hocks and hold the scents of glandular secretions and urine.

The breeding season of both species occurs from October to late November, with a concentration of activity in early November. Approximately seven months after mating the doe gives birth, often to twin fawns. She caches her young among heavy growth to safeguard them from predators while she feeds on a variety of herbs, grasses, and deciduous growth. As with other ungulates, winter starvation is the largest cause of death.

OPPOSITE: Dry montane forest of lodgepole pine, Douglas-fir, aspen, and alder north of Cache Creek.

RIGHT: Mule deer are found throughout most of the province. Spike antlers are found on young bucks and poorly nourished individuals.

No other native North American duck is as brilliantly coloured as the wood duck. The breeding plumage of drakes consists of a glossy green and purple head with white stripes, which vividly contrasts the mottled burgundy breast, white belly, and iridescent wing and tail feathers. Particularly distinctive are the long, slicked-backed crest, orange-red eyes, and red and white bill.

In British Columbia the breeding range of the wood duck is restricted to southern areas of the province. Mated pairs search for a nesting site in tree cavities or woodpecker holes. The female lays between 8-15 eggs in a cushion of down and incubates them for approximately one month. After hatching, the ducklings, coaxed by their mother's persistent, whistle-like call, leap from their nest cavity, plummeting as much as 15 metres to the forest floor. Protected by a thick layer of down, they usually bounce, land unharmed, and follow their mother to a nearby pond or lake.

During their first few weeks, the ducklings eat a high protein diet of insects. Adult fare is 90 percent plants, particularly duckweed, grasses, and pondweeds. The wood duck's feeding habits are distinctive in that it consumes more fruits and nuts than any other North American duck.

OPPOSITE: Night falls on the Columbia River in the Rocky Mountains near Golden.

LEFT: A male wood duck preens its spectacular plumage.

Mergansers are diving ducks adapted for swimming under water and catching fish. Their streamlined bodies and large, webbed feet with lobed, hind toes enable them to pursue a variety of swimming prey. Small fish, frogs, and newts, although slippery, are easily grasped and held in their long, serrated, hooked bills. Like other diving ducks, mergansers have short legs which are positioned far to the rear of their bodies to facilitate diving and underwater propulsion.

Three species of mergansers are found in British Columbia. Although most are conspicuously crested, they display significant differences in plumage, size, and breeding range. The common merganser is the largest and breeds throughout the province. Drakes are particularly distinctive in nuptial plumage with contrasting black and white bodies and iridescent green heads. The red-breasted merganser is a smaller, medium-sized duck with a conspicuous, thin, double crest. Although it is the most common winter merganser on the Pacific coast, it only breeds in the far northwestern corner of the province. Unlike other mergansers which nest in hollow trees, it prefers to nest on the ground. The smallest merganser in the province is the hooded merganser. Its size is more than compensated for by its flashy plumage. Males have a large, white crest that opens like a fan during courtship displays. Hooded mergansers breed throughout the southern half of the province.

LEFT: Lac Le Jeune near Kamloops is one of the many small lakes of the interior.

OPPOSITE: A female common merganser churns through still waters on a fishing foray.

PAGE 126: The thin, pointed trees of the subalpine forest have a growth form adapted to shed heavy, mountain snowfall.

PAGE 127: A Rocky Mountain bighorn lamb nibbles a grass stem.

PLANTS OF THE INTERIOR FORESTS

TREES	SHRUBS/FERNS	WILDFLOWERS

Columbian Forest

Western red cedar	Devil's club	Bunchberry
Western hemlock	False azalea	Foam flower
Douglas-fir	False box	Twisted stalk
Western larch	Red elderberry	Twinflower
Engelmann spruce	Black twinberry	Skunk cabbage
White spruce	Salmonberry	Cow parsnip
Western yew	Thimbleberry	Mountain lily
Bitter cherry	Kinnikinnick	Queen's cup
	Lady fern	Pipsissewa

Montane Forest

Douglas-fir	Saskatoon berry	Delphinium
Lodgepole pine	Tall Oregon grape	Scarlet gilia
Ponderosa pine	Kinnikinnick	Balsam root sunflower
Trembling aspen	Blue elderberry	Mariposa lily
	Squaw currant	Yellow fritillary
	Soopolallie	Yarrow
	Woodsia fern	Blue Jacob's ladder

Subalpine Forest

Engelmann spruce	Black mountain	Indian hellebore
White spruce	huckleberry	Mountain valerian
Mountain hemlock	Kinnikinnick	Broad-leaved lupine
Alpine fir	Sitka mountain ash	Western columbine
Lodgepole pine	Black twinberry	Fireweed
Alpine larch	Soopolallie	Meadow spirea
Whitebark pine	Oval-leaved blueberry	Indian paintbrush
Trembling aspen	Bracken fern	False lady's slipper
		Mountain daisy

ANIMALS OF THE INTERIOR FORESTS

MAMMALS

Rocky Mountain
  bighorn sheep
Moose
Mule deer
Grizzly bear
Black bear
Fisher
Marten
Wolf
Porcupine
Red squirrel
Yellow-bellied marmot
Golden-mantled ground
  squirrel

BIRDS

American kestrel
Pygmy owl
Saw-whet owl
Ruffed grouse
American dipper
Cedar waxwing
Mourning dove
Red crossbill
Mountain bluebird
Pine siskin
Western flycatcher
Pygmy nuthatch

OTHER ANIMALS

Rubber boa
Wood frog

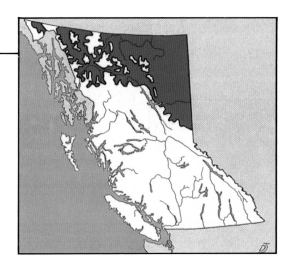

CHAPTER 5

THE NORTHERN FORESTS

Remote and vast, the northern third of British Columbia is clothed in a seemingly endless, mottled green blanket of coniferous trees. Here temperatures and precipitation are generally lower than in the interior forests to the south. Bordering the arctic tundra, this northern, or boreal, forest is part of a continuous evergreen band 800 to 1500 kilometres wide, stretching nearly from coast to coast. The severe climate together with the poor soils results in a frozen, sombre landscape—a mosaic of spired conifers, matchstick stands of aspen, networks of rushing, poplar-lined rivers, and a myriad of dark bogs and pristine lakes.

Boreal Forest

The boreal forest is primarily coniferous. White and black spruce are the dominant species, with lodgepole pine and alpine fir common in mountainous areas. Black spruce has one great advantage over other trees in not only reproducing by seed but also by developing on its lower branches roots which eventually grow into new trees. Trembling aspen and birch, two species which replace spruce after forest fires, as well as larch, brighten this wilderness. Unlike other evergreens, larch has needles which turn from green to a glowing yellow in late autumn before dropping.

Tracts of boreal forest stretch unbroken for hundreds of miles—dense, dark places where the pervasive greyish-green silence is interrupted only infrequently by the lone call of a loon or the fall of a spruce cone. The interlaced, evergreen canopy allows little sunlight to reach the understorey. Over the years fallen needles accumulate on the forest floor, smothering and acidifying the soil. Only a few plants, like bunchberry and twinflower, have adapted to these soils and the permafrost that is found in the more northern regions of the boreal forest.

Wetlands

In low-lying areas of poor drainage, the stretch of trees is broken by muskeg or spruce bogs—black, acid waters overlain with springy mats of sphagnum moss. Rimmed by black spruce and larch, these highly acidic environments harbour a distinct community of plants. Scrub willows, birches, Labrador tea, and small cranberry are common. The latter two shrubs have adapted to cold, dry winds by growing a woolly layer of insulating hairs on the undersurface of their leaves. Another distinctive plant, the carnivorous sundew, survives by preying on insects. They supply the plant with nitrogen and phosphorous, vital elements it cannot secure from the poor soil.

The northern forests are stippled with many small lakes, rich sloughs, and potholes occurring in depressions left behind by the retreating glaciers. Although the vegetation of these wetlands is of little benefit to man, it is vital to wildlife, providing both food and shelter. The cattails and bulrushes bordering lakes and sloughs attract nesting ducks, geese, swans, loons, and huge flocks of red-winged blackbirds. Water smartweed is another valuable aquatic plant. Its seeds constitute about 25 percent of the diet of many species of waterfowl. The berries of red osier dogwood, a widespread wetland shrub, are equally important to songbirds. Even the moose, the largest of all deer, ventures into these northern lakes to feed on aquatic vegetation rich in sodium salts.

Wildlife

The northern woods are home for many species of birds and mammals that once thrived in areas to the south, now crowded with humans. The wild, forgotten landscape provides undisturbed habitat for many large carnivores including black and grizzly bears, wolves, marten, fisher, and lynx. Small herbivores characteristic of the region are the tundra red-backed vole, the arctic heather vole, and the varying hare.

In the brief interlude of summer the courtship songs of kinglets, chickadees, thrushes, and warblers filter through the forest canopy. Boreal chickadees, hooded and common mergansers, bufflehead ducks, and woodpeckers rear their young in the cavities of old trees while Bonaparte's gulls build their nests in tree boughs. Well adapted to long winters, northern chickadees store food under the bark of branches that are above the winter snow cover but below boughs exposed to blizzards. Other year long residents are the great-horned owl and the great grey owl. Silent, nighttime hunters, they have rangey, sinewy bodies insulated against the unforgiving cold by several inches of down and feathers. A smaller, robin-sized raptor, the boreal owl, also hunts the northern woods, its acute binocular vision seeking out small rodents.

In the northeastern corner of the province the boreal forest covers a huge plateau, an extension of the Great Plains of the prairie provinces and states. Known as the Peace River Country, parts of this region have undergone extensive agricultural and industrial development—most recently the gargantuan coal mining project at Tumbler Ridge. Terrain not altered by human activity is characterized in many places by parklands dominated by pure stands of trembling aspen. This corner of the province, lying as it does outside British Columbia's curtain of mountains, hosts a number of birds normally associated with the fauna of eastern Canada, including the ovenbird, Connecticut warbler, common grackle, blue jay, and rose-breasted grosbeak.

PAGE 128: White spruce and balsam poplar on a dry hillside in the boreal forest in spring.

OPPOSITE: Moose can run at speeds of almost 60 kilometres an hour.

The moose (preceding page) is the largest member of the deer family, measuring up to two metres high at the shoulder and weighing as much as a professional baseball team. Ranging throughout British Columbia east of the Coast Mountains, moose are particularly well adapted to life in the boreal forest. Aided by long legs and broad hooves, they can step through the deep snows of the northern woods and forage in the soggy bottoms of marshes.

Like most other large animals, moose are herbivorous, feeding on a wide variety of trees and shrubs, including the twigs and bark of willow, dogwood, aspen, birch, and balsam fir. In early spring they graze on tender, new grasses by wristing (the front-legged version of kneeling) on the ground. Because their winter diet is low in salt, they spend the summer wading and swimming in lakes and rivers in search of sodium-rich pondweeds and water lilies. They even dive up to five metres to pull up aquatic vegetation. By autumn bulls reach maximum size, increasing their weight by almost a third, and sporting antlers two metres across that can weigh half as much as a man.

A slender tree, trembling aspen is common throughout the province east of the Coast Range, preferring open, well-drained sites. Its name is derived from the fine-toothed, long-stemmed leaves which rustle with the slightest breeze. The trunk is smooth, creamy white, and marked by dark, warty patches. Strips of missing aspen bark are a sign that elk have been feeding. Although aspens yield an abundance of buoyant, wind-dispersed seeds, many groves are propagated by spreading root systems which send up new saplings. Pure stands of large aspen are common in the Peace River region.

RIGHT: A grove of snow-dusted aspens in the Peace River parklands.

The secretive and nocturnal habits of the lynx make sightings of this small feline rare. Lynx are at home in the boreal forest where their luxurious, salt and pepper coats blend in with the gloomy, coniferous vegetation. Broad, padded paws, as large as saucers, function like snowshoes, enabling the lynx to roam the northern forests with ease.

Adult lynx only come together during the breeding season in early spring. After a gestation period of two months, two to five kittens are born in a hollow log or under thick brush. The young remain under the protection of their mother through the first winter.

The great dependency of the lynx on the varying hare, its chief prey, leaves it vulnerable to the hare's well known, cyclic, population fluctuations. When hares are plentiful, lynx numbers climb accordingly. A single cat may kill 200 hares a year. When hares are scarce, lynx populations decline. Deer, young caribou and moose, birds, and various small mammals supplement the lynx's diet.

OPPOSITE: A solitary hunter, the lynx is a creature of the forests, with its centre of abundance in the north-central part of the province.

LEFT: White spruce and trembling aspen are common associates of the northern forests.

The northern woods are home to North America's largest owl, the great grey. This raptor is distinguished by a wing span of 1.5 metres, long tail, and large, grey facial disk. Armed with needle-sharp talons and a powerful, hooked beak, it tops the food chain of the boreal forest.

Often seen hunting from a low perch, the great grey owl relies on acute hearing and binocular vision to locate its prey. It can detect mice and voles under a seemingly sound-proof, opaque blanket of snow. Plunging down on its prey with talons spread wide, it clamps lethally onto its victim. Small prey is swallowed whole, and large animals are sheared into chunks. A few hours after the owl has fed, the indigestible fur and bones are compacted in the stomach into golf ball size pellets and regurgitated.

Owls lay their eggs in the unused nests of other birds or in tree cavities. As with most birds of prey, incubation begins as soon as the first egg is laid. As a result, the clutch hatches out over a number of days, producing significant size differences among the young. At each feeding the oldest nestling is filled up first. In times of plenty all the young receive adequate nutrition, but in lean years only the largest survive.

OPPOSITE: A bird of the northern forests, the great grey owl occasionally ventures into southern British Columbia, possibly due to food shortage on its home range. The hearing of some owls is so sensitive that prey can be located and killed in complete darkness.

LEFT: Black cottonwood is widespread in British Columbia. Pure stands are usually found along river banks or other moist, low-lying areas.

Through the centuries the wolf has been a feared and misunderstood animal. Eliminated from much of its original range by shooting and poisoning, it is now largely confined to remote, unsettled regions of the province.

Wolves are among the most social of all mammals. Organizing into packs of less than ten individuals, they have a stable social order based on a dominant breeding pair. Although the top-ranking, or "alpha", male and female prevent others from breeding, the young are fed and cared for by the entire pack. Often unmated aunts and uncles guard and play with the young while the parents are hunting. Pack cooperation enables the wolves to hunt down animals much larger than themselves. Killing mainly deer and moose, wolf packs often split up and ambush their prey.

Protective of their own close-knit family, wolves can be fiercely hostile to other packs and lone wolves which invade their territory. Urination posts mark borders and warn intruders against trespassing. Like other misconceptions about the wolf, howling is not an expression of melancholy but another way of maintaining pack unity and defining territory.

LEFT: A young wolf peers cautiously out of the underbrush. It is cared for not only by its mother and father but aunts and uncles as well.

OPPOSITE: Lodgepole pine, spruce, willow, and aspen blanket a valley in the Cassiar Mountains. (**Photo: Fred Chapman**)

Although once common on the Great Plains of North America, the grizzly now survives only in the western mountains and northern tundra regions of Canada and the United States. Standing taller on its hind legs than a man and weighing as much as half a dozen refrigerators, large grizzlies have no enemies aside from humans. Unfortunately even these magnificent carnivores are no match for the bulldozers, chainsaws, and high explosives that threaten their survival.

A low reproductive rate and a shy, reclusive nature make the grizzly especially vulnerable to human disturbance. Females do not reach sexual maturity until they are five years old, and litters are small—usually one or two cubs. The young stay with the sow for at least two years during which time she does not breed. Industries like logging and mining not only limit suitable denning sites, they psychologically stress the population with consequent negatiave impacts on reproductive and feeding success.

The Khutzeymateen Valley north of Prince Rupert, a wilderness area with considerable numbers of grizzlies, is being considered by the provincial government for ecological reserve status, a move that would give some protection to the beleaguered grizzly.

LEFT: In the province's interior, grizzlies range the higher altitudes searching for berries during the summer and fall. A large bear gains more than 200 kilograms before hibernating.

OPPOSITE: Autumn on the remote Spatsizi Plateau. (**Photo: Fred Chapman**)

Leading a semi-aquatic lifestyle, the muskrat (*overleaf*) is common in the many lakes, rivers, and ponds of the boreal forest. Its dense, waterproof coat is composed of a soft, air-trapping inner pelt and an outer layer of course guard hairs. Equipped with partially webbed, hind feet and a long, flattened, rudder-like tail, muskrats can swim at least 100 metres under water and remain submerged for more than 15 minutes.

These large rodents are mainly herbivorous, feeding on the roots, tubers, stems, and leaves of a variety of aquatic and terrestrial plants. Muskrats can seal their lips behind their prominent incisors, freeing these chisel-like teeth to gnaw at underwater vegetation without taking in water.

Like beavers, muskrats are masterful architects and builders. They use their long claws to dig bank burrows with underwater entrances. Winter lodges, which can be home to more than a dozen muskrats, are built of cattails, bulrushes, and pondweeds piled into a large mound that is plastered together with mud. Inside, several nesting chambers are hollowed out of the vegetation. Here females produce two or three litters of six to eight young each year.

One of the many ducks that breed in the Peace River parklands, a blue-winged teal springs into flight. To become airborne it thrusts against the water with its feet and wings.

PLANTS AND ANIMALS OF THE NORTHERN FORESTS

TREES	SHRUBS/FERNS	WILDFLOWERS
White spruce	Labrador tea	Northern asphodel
Black spruce	Squashberry	Bunchberry
Alpine fir	Canada blueberry	Fireweed
Lodgepole pine	Saskatoon berry	Arctic raspberry
Western larch	Dwarf huckleberry	Strawberry blight
Trembling aspen	Red osier dogwood	Ladies' tresses
Balsam poplar	Scrub birch	Sundew
Sandbar willow	Kinnikinnick	Yellow violet
Paper birch	Small cranberry	Yellow pond lily
	Swamp laurel	
	Crowberry	
	Bracken fern	

MAMMALS	BIRDS	OTHER ANIMALS
Thinhorn sheep	Great grey owl	Chorus frog
Grizzly bear	Boreal owl	Long-toed salamander
Black bear	Northern hawk owl	
Wolf	Northern shrike	
Coyote	Northern three-toed	
Lynx	woodpecker	
Beaver	Common grackle	
Porcupine	Ovenbird	
Muskrat	Blue jay	
Varying hare	White-winged crossbill	
Tundra red-backed vole	Golden-crowned kinglet	
	Bonaparte's gull	
	Blue-winged teal	

OPPOSITE: The spotted sandpiper is a common breeder along the wetlands of the Peace River parklands.

TOP LEFT: A dainty shrub, swamp laurel is commonly found in bogs through most of British Columbia. The leaves and flowers contain andromedotoxin, a compound poisonous to cattle and sheep.

BOTTOM LEFT: A muskrat munches of a cattail tuber, its main food. Cattail leaves and stems also are used to build its winter lodges.

CHAPTER 6

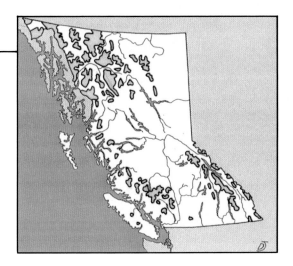

THE ALPINE

The alpine zone is found in the highest mountain regions throughout the province at elevations where normal tree growth is prevented by severe climatic factors. This is the harshest of British Columbia's life zones combining long, cold winters, strong winds, and short growing seasons lasting as little as 25 days in some areas. Temperatures can drop to below freezing at any time of the year, and summer blizzards are not uncommon. Despite the severe weather, many plants and animals survive and exhibit intriguing adaptations to life at high elevations.

Due to the floral displays of the high country meadows, the abundance and easy visibility of wildlife, and the magnificent wilderness vistas, British Columbia's alpine areas are popular destinations of outdoor enthusiasts. Although most regions are remote and inaccessible, a few are easily reached by car and a short hike or ride up a ski lift. One can drive into the extensive, rolling subalpine meadows of Manning Park in the Cascade Range and to the summit of Mount Revelstoke in the Columbia Mountains. A chairlift at Whistler Mountain north of Vancouver is open during the summer to carry visitors into the alpine meadows.

Alpine vegetation follows a ragged but undeniable pattern—the higher the elevation, the more dwarfed and sparse the plant life becomes. Although by definition the zone is treeless, at timberline are found the struggling remnants of the thick forests of the lower slopes. Limber pine, Engelmann spruce, alpine fir, and mountain hemlock are likely to survive here as bent and twisted dwarfs known as krummholz. Their stunted growth form is a response to poor soil conditions, high winds, and heavy snow loading for most of the year, although in sheltered soil pockets they retain a normal if smaller form.

Subalpine Meadows

Just above treeline the terrain opens into rolling, lush

meadows. Here conditions of ample moisture from melting snow packs, intense sunlight unfiltered by trees, and gentler slopes produce spectacular wildflower displays. These plants grow at an amazing rate—flowering, reproducing, and storing food for the next year in the few weeks of an alpine summer. Bursting upwards using stored energy from their thickened underground stems, glacier lilies and western anemones are among the first to bloom. In frantic profusion others soon follow—lupines, arnicas, paintbrushes, and daisies to name a few. Most species exhibit obvious adaptations to the harsh environment. Some, like western anemone and alpine cinquefoil, have large disk-shaped flowerheads which act as miniature solar collectors to accelerate development of seeds. The stems and leaves of many herbs are overgrown with insulating hairs, protection from the scathing winds that cause extreme heat and moisture loss by evaporation.

Above the meadows conditions grow abruptly more severe; soils become thinner, slopes steepen and grow more rocky, temperatures fall, and run-off of precious moisture is accelerated drastically. Nevertheless some life survives here. There are tough, scraggly plants with creeping growth forms and small, thick, moisture-retaining leaves—both adaptations to the high winds and low temperatures of these exposed heights. For a few weeks in summer two common shrubs, red and white moss heather, enliven the terrain with their tiny, bell-shaped blooms. Clinging to the dry, barren ridges are cushions of mat-forming plants like spreading phlox and moss campion. As one continues toward the summit, the last and least of the plants are found on the rocks—crusts of multi-hued lichens. The highest reaches of the alpine zone are barren, ice-capped peaks devoid of life.

Wildlife

The birds of the alpland are few but distinctive. Most sought after by bird watchers, yet most difficult to find, is the white-tailed ptarmigan. Its mottled summer plumage blends in so well with surrounding rocks and vegetation that often the only clue to its whereabouts is a soft, low hoot. Superbly adapted to its environment, the ptarmigan's dense feathers grow right down to its toes providing insulation against the bitter cold. Near the treeline a noisy, grey, robin-sized bird, the Clark's nutcracker, feeds on the seeds of pine cones. Hummingbirds also frequent the alpine meadows attracted by the fiery blooms of Indian paintbrush, red monkey flower, and western columbine.

The lofty, alpine reaches provide excellent opportunities for viewing mammals. Elk, deer, caribou, and black and grizzly bears migrate up to the meadows during the summer. Feasting on herbaceous growth and berries, they gain considerable weight, mostly fat, to sustain them through the winter months usually spent at lower altitudes. A grizzly gains as much as 200 kilograms during a summer of high altitude grazing. Ground squirrels and marmots are permanent residents. To escape the cold they hibernate or simply sleep for eight to ten months a year in burrows buried metres under the snow. Another small resident, the pika, busies itself during the summer harvesting hay, curing it in the warm sun, and storing it in sheltered places for winter use. Special characteristics of the mountain goat permit it to remain active in the alpine zone throughout the year.

PAGE 146: These distinctive peaks of the Coast Range near Vancouver are known as 'The Lions'.

OPPOSITE: In summer blue grouse move into alpine meadows with their half-grown young to feed on insects and berries.

Mountain goats inhabit the steepest, roughest, and coldest terrain in the province. Short, muscular legs, non-skid soles, and highly flexible toes enable them to negotiate vertical rock faces where few other animals dare to venture. These agile members of the antelope family nonchalantly leap as far as three metres over rock chasms that may be several hundred metres deep.

During the summer, mountain goats frequent the lush alpine meadows to feed on a variety of grasses, herbs, and woody plants. Deep, winter snow forces them to abandon the high alpine for lower elevations where plant growth is more exposed. Here they graze on conifers and paw through the thin snows to reach lichens, mosses, and other plants. While wandering for good grazing, many goats are seriously lamed or killed by avalanches and rock slides.

After snowmelt the nannies give birth to one, but sometimes two, and rarely three, kids. In this rough and inhospitable terrain the mother is extremely protective of her young for the first year—guarding them from falls, leading them to fresh grazing, and thwarting attacks from predators such as golden eagles. For added protection nannies and kids congregate in nursery herds. The billies seek out these maternal bands during the rutting season in November.

LEFT: Mountain goats inhabit remote, mountainous regions of the province. They are insulated from the harsh climate by thick, ice-repellent wool.

OPPOSITE: These steep, angular peaks in the Purcell Range near Golden provide only scant and scattered footholds for plants. Scars from the footsteps of hikers may take decades and even centuries to heal.

The largest of all North American squirrels, the hoary marmot is superbly adapted for alpine life, sleeping underground throughout the long, cold winter and packing a year's worth of eating, growth, and activity into a few, short, summer months. After emerging from hibernation in late April, the males compete to secure the best territories and thereby attract a harem of females. One month after mating, the female produces a litter of four to five young. Her offspring do not reach sexual maturity until they are two to three years old, remaining in her care for most of this time. Colonial protection is also important. While sun-bathing near their burrows or feeding in the open, rolling alpland, marmots are vulnerable to predators like golden eagles or bears. When a marmot spots a predator, it emits a loud, police-like whistle to warn the entire colony.

In order to survive seven or eight months of hibernation, marmots store considerable fat in their intestines and in cushioning layers around their bodies. Throughout the summer they feed on the lush vegetation of alpine meadows, gorging on wildflowers, grasses, and berries. By fall their body weight increases by as much as 20 percent with some individuals attaining a weight of 14 kilograms. The last to enter hibernation are the females which require a longer period to build up fat reserves.

TOP LEFT: A small member of the rabbit family, the Rocky Mountain pika inhabits talus slopes near suitable food sources from sea level to above timberline.

BOTTOM LEFT: A female hoary marmot and her offspring pose warily near their burrow entrance in the Cascade Mountains.

OPPOSITE: The lower, less rugged mountains of Vancouver Island are dwarfed by the ice-capped peaks of the Coast Range in the background.

Although many hikers are lured up to alpine heights by the beauty of the flowers, the colourful display is intended to impress not man but insects. Most flowers rely on insects, and sometimes birds, to achieve pollination. These airborne couriers are lured to the blooms from considerable distance by bright colours and enticing perfumes. Once they arrive, the flower treats them to a feast of nectar and pollen. While feeding, the insects bump into the stamens, knocking off pollen that adheres to their bodies and is later deposited, again unwittingly, on the pistil which results in fertilization.

The prevalence of yellow in many alpine blooms—cinquefoil, buttercup, glacier lily, wood betony, daisy, arnica—is an indication that this colour is highly visible to many insects. The monkey flower directs pollinators toward its nectar with a pattern of leading lines. A number of red flowers, like paintbrush and columbine, have blooms that can be probed most effectively by the long bill and tongue of a hummingbird. Red has become so alluring that a high country hiker wearing a red sweater is likely to be buzzed frequently by hungry hummingbirds. Bees favour blue, and it is interesting that access to the nectar reservoir of a species like the blue lupine can only be gained by a strong, heavy-bodied insect like the bumblebee.

OPPOSITE TOP LEFT: Meadows above timberline explode with brilliantly coloured wildflowers such as buttercup and glacier lily during the brief summer.

OPPOSITE BOTTOM LEFT: The deep azure of a sweep of flowering lupines has enlivened the trek of many a tired mountain hiker.

OPPOSITE RIGHT: Indian paintbrush is jostled by the wind in a meadow near timberline. Its scarlet blooms are actually modified leaves.

RIGHT: Rogers Pass in the Selkirk Mountains.

PLANTS AND ANIMALS OF THE ALPINE

DWARFED TREES

Alpine fir
Mountain hemlock
Limber pine
Engelmann spruce

SHRUBS/FERNS

Dwarf juniper
Dwarf willow
Black mountain
   huckleberry
Dwarf blueberry
Oval-leaved blueberry
Trailing azalea
White moss heather
Red heather
Alpine lady fern

WILDFLOWERS

Broad-leaved arnica
Alpine cinquefoil
Western columbine
Mountain daisy
Globe flower
Indian paintbrush
Broad-leaved lupine
Mountain valerian
Red monkey flower
Glacier lily
Western anemone
Elephant's head
Wood betony
Wild tiger lily
Lyall's rock cress

MAMMALS

Mountain caribou
Elk
Mountain goat
Black bear
Grizzly bear
Hoary marmot
Vancouver Island
   marmot
Rocky mountain pika
Columbian ground
   squirrel
Least chipmunk

BIRDS

Golden eagle
Blue grouse
White-tailed ptarmigan
Clark's nutcracker
Common raven
Gray jay
Gray-crowned rosy finch
Golden-crowned
   sparrow
Rufous hummingbird

LEFT: A Columbian ground squirrel dines on rock plants in an alpine meadow in the Rockies. These animals hibernate for almost eight months of the year.

OPPOSITE LEFT: The large, moppy seedheads of western anemone give rise to the popular name, tow-head babies.

OPPOSITE RIGHT: Masses of red monkey flowers thrive along mountain streams and on gentle slopes where there is seepage from melting snow packs.

SELECTED BIBLIOGRAPHY

Bandoni, R.J. and A.F. Szczawinski. 1964. *Guide to Common Mushrooms of British Columbia* (Handbook Series No. 24). Victoria: British Columbia Provincial Museum.

Banfield, A.W.F. 1974. *The Mammals of Canada.* Toronto: University of Toronto Press.

Barker, M.L. 1977. *Natural Resources of British Columbia and the Yukon.* Vancouver: Douglas, David & Charles and Newton Abbot and England: David & Charles.

Bodsworth, F. 1970. *The Pacific Coast.* Toronto: Natural Science of Canada Limited.

Bryant, L. 1982. *British Columbia—This Favoured Land.* Vancouver and Toronto: Douglas & McIntyre.

Clark, L.J. and J.G. Trelawny. ed. 1976. *Wildflowers of the Pacific Northwest: From Alaska to Northern California.* Sidney, British Columbia: Gray's Publishing Company.

Clifford, C.G. 1966. *Amphibians of British Columbia* (Handbook Series No. 2). Victoria: British Columbia Provincial Museum.

——. 1966. *Guide to Marine Life of British Columbia* (Handbook Series No.21). Victoria: British Columbia Provincial Museum.

——. 1960. *Guide to Reptiles of British Columbia* (Handbook Series No. 3). Victoria: British Columbia Provincial Museum.

Edwards, R.Y. 1970. *The Mountain Barrier.* Toronto: Natural Science of Canada Limited.

Farley, A.L. 1979. *Atlas of British Columbia.* Vancouver: University of British Columbia Press.

Fitzharris, T.R. 1983. *The Island: A Natural History of Vancouver Island.* Toronto: Oxford University Press.

Haig-Brown, R. 1961. *The Living Land: An Account of the Natural Resources of British Columbia.* Toronto: The McMillan Company of Canada Limited.

Hitchcock, C.L. and A. Cronquist. 1973. *Flora of the Pacific Northwest.* Seattle: University of Washington Press.

Islands Protection Society. 1984. *Islands at the Edge: Preserving the Queen Charlotte Islands Wilderness.* Vancouver and Toronto: Douglas & McIntyre and Seattle and London: University of Washington Press.

Lyons, C.P. 1965. *Trees, Shrubs and Flowers to Know in British Columbia.* Toronto: J.M. Dent & Sons Limited.

McTaggart-Cowan, I. and C.J. Guiget. 1956. *The Mammals of British Columbia.* (Handbook Series No. 11). Victoria: British Columbia Provincial Museum.

Ricketts, E.F. and J. Calvin. 1962. *Between Pacific Tides.* California: Stanford Unviersity Press.

Savage, A. and C. Savage. 1981. *Wild Mammals of Western Canada.* Saskatoon, Saskatchewan: Western Producer Prairie Books.

Smith, I. 1978. *The Unknown Island.* Vancouver: Douglas & McIntyre.

Terres, J.K. 1980. *The Audubon Society Encyclopedia of North American Birds.* New York: Alfred A. Knopf Inc.

Young, C. 1985. *The Forests of British Columbia.* North Vancouver: Whitecap Books.

OPPOSITE: Sunset over the Selkirk Mountains near Revelstoke.

INDEX OF PLATES